# DIVORCE: THE CHILD'S POINT OF VIEW

# DIVORCE: THE CHILD'S POINT OF VIEW

Yvette Walczak with Sheila Burns

**Harper & Row, Publishers**
London

Cambridge  San Francisco
Hagerstown Mexico City
Philadelphia São Paulo
New York Sydney

Copyright © 1984 Yvette Walczak and Sheila Burns
All rights reserved

First published 1984

Harper & Row Publishers Ltd
28 Tavistock Street
London WC2E 7PN

British Library Cataloguing in Publication Data
Burns, Shelia
    Divorce: the child's point of view.
    1. Divorce      2. Children of divorced parents
    I. Title    II. Walczak, Yvette
    306.8'9     HQ814

    ISBN 0–06–318278–5

Typeset by Activity Ltd, Salisbury, Wilts.
Printed and bound by Butler & Tanner Ltd, Frome and London

## About the authors

**Yvette Walczak** was born in Poland and has lived in England since 1946. She graduated in sociology from the London School of Economics in 1954 and trained in social work at the Institute of Medical Social Work and the Tavistock Clinic. She has worked in a number of different hospitals and for the Family Welfare Association. She currently practises as a Family Therapist on a part-time basis and works as a volunteer in a day centre for the mentally ill. She is a Senior Lecturer in Social Work at the Polytechnic of North London. She has two daughters.

**Sheila Burns** is a Senior Lecturer in Social Work at the Polytechnic of North London. She was previously employed as a Child Care Officer in the City of Westminster Children's Department. She is an active member of Families Need Fathers, Society for Equal Parental Rights, of which she was Honorary Secretary for three years and also edited the news letter. She is married with three step-children.

# CONTENTS

*To all those who took part in this study, with our gratitude*

## Acknowledgements

This book could not have been written without the generous help of all the children and adults who took part in the project. We are grateful to them for their time, interest, and the trust they placed in us. We should also like to thank the parents of children under eighteen for their consent, their hospitality, and willingness to be excluded from the interviews.

Many friends and colleagues at the Polytechnic of North London and in the Department of Family and Child Psychiatry, Queen Elizabeth Hospital for Children, offered us much-needed support, advice, and helpful criticism. They are too numerous to be listed by name. We can only mention Dr Paul Corrigan, Dr Constance Dennehy and Ms. Jean Snelling.

The manuscript was typed by Mrs Pat Howe, Mrs Peggy Riddle, Mrs Joan Slingsby and members of the typing pool of the Polytechnic of North London. We are not only grateful to them for offering their typing skills, but also for their sustained interest in the project.

Jim Ring, a social statistician, was responsible for analysing the data. His statistical expertise, advice, and support throughout the duration of the project were invaluable and the data could not have been gathered, studied, and presented without his participation. We should like to express to him our warmest thanks.

We are also greatly indebted to our research assistant, Ms. Louise Klinger, who was involved both in collecting and analysing the data. Her interviewing skills were a great asset in such a sensitive area as parental divorce. We should like to express our thanks and gratitude to Ms. Naomi Roth of Harper and Row for her invaluable editorial work on the manuscript and to Stephen Corcoran who compiled the index.

The project was financed by the Polytechnic of North London.

# INTRODUCTION

'And what is the use of a book', thought Alice, 'without pictures or conversation?'

(Lewis Carroll, *Alice's Adventures in Wonderland*)

This book is about children and divorce. It is based on 'conversations'- as Alice might have described them – with the children of divorced parents. It describes their experiences and conveys their points of view on divorce.

At the time of parental separation all the children were under eighteen years old. When we talked to them, fifty were still under eighteen and fifty were adults. The children and adolescents shared with us their recent and current experiences. The adults offered childhood memories combined with mature insight. The pictures they all painted were mental images. Some of them were blurred, but most were vivid memories of family outings and scenes of violence which had left a particularly strong impression. Other images were of parents sadly standing on the doorstep when visiting children with whom they no longer shared a home. We were told about the relief and misery which were felt simultaneously by many children when they first learned that their parents were splitting up. They had taken it for granted that the marriage was permanent and 'ordinary', whatever it had been like. Most children had hoped that one day their parents would stop fighting and arguing and get on well together. Divorce had not been envisaged even as an end to strife.

We were told how children learn about separation, custody and access arrangements and of some of the consequences of divorce such as changes in financial circumstances and in relationships within the post-divorce family. A variety of short-term and long-term consequences were described.

There are many reasons for embarking on research, amongst them natural human curiosity, awareness of social trends, the wish to test the validity of established and influential views on important issues, eagerness for new knowledge where there appear to be gaps. Last, but not least, the personal history of researchers themselves may influence their interests and concerns. All these factors formed the background to the current study.

We are all involved in family life in some way, yet little is known about many aspects of it. As we walk down the street any of us may have wondered what goes on behind the closed doors of homes inhabited by 'ordinary' families. Family life is shrouded in secrecy and regarded as private. Often it is only when a family is in trouble that the secrets are revealed to the outside world and new insight gained. Many adults believe that it is good to have secrets inside the family as well as those kept from the outside world. Parents who follow the old maxim 'not in front of the children' more often than not leave their children in a position of 'half-knowing', feeling bewildered and mystified when suitable explanations could dispel fear and fantasy. As we were convinced that children know and understand a great deal more than adults give them credit for we wished to explore this further. We regarded children as a valuable source of information about themselves and their families.

Divorce has become an important social trend and feature of family life especially since the Divorce Reform Act, 1969, became law in January 1971. Divorce has become an easier and more usual solution to an unhappy marriage than ever before. Every year not only a great number of adults, but also children, are involved in divorce. According to official statistics[1] in 1980, 157,000 marriages were dissolved in the United Kingdom. Sixty percent of divorcing couples had children under sixteen, thus involving 155,000 children. Of these just under a quarter were under five, just under half between five and ten and just over half between eleven and sixteen. Half the couples divorce after they have been married for between five and fourteen years, and while the children are still young. These figures represent complex human situations.

There is no consensus of opinion among child care experts about divorce or post-divorce arrangements. Some believe that parents should stay together at almost any cost for the sake of their children.[2] Others conclude that an unhappy marriage is more harmful to child development than divorce per se.[3] As regards post-divorce arrangements, some advocate restricted or no contact with the non-custodial parent,[4] while others consider post-divorce contact with both parents to be the most beneficial arrangement.[5] There is a growing body of opinion which supports this view, and which believes that it is the task of parents and the whole of society to facilitate this arrangement. Our own findings lend support to this view of parenting after divorce.

There is a large gap in our knowledge about the child's view of divorce; this is apparent in classical literature, modern fiction, films, television, sociological and psychological studies. The focus has mainly been on adult experiences. Tolstoy, in *Anna Karenina*,[6] brilliantly portrays the sadness and despair of a mother who is banned from her husband's home and the husband's anger which leads him to pretend to his son that the mother is dead. Little is revealed about the child's feelings. *Kramer* v. *Kramer*[7] is a book about three people, Joanna, Ted and Billy. It portrays Ted's and Joanna's love, anger and frustration with their situation and each other. Although references are made to Billy's concern about the lack of peanut butter sandwiches after his mother is gone, his pleasure at seeing her after prolonged absence and his wish, that his parents should remarry most of the time, we do not know what is going through Billy's mind while the spotlight is on the adults.

Sociological investigations have also concentrated on the experiences of adults, and the children's reactions are seen only through the eyes of parents and child care experts.[8]

As social workers, we have come into contact with many divorcing couples and have been concerned about the arrangements for the care of the children. The law requires that a judge should be satisfied with the arrangements being made for the children by their parents before granting a divorce. In all contested custody cases (which form only a small proportion of all cases involving children) the judge himself makes a decision, sometimes taking into account a Court Welfare Officer's report. This means that a Court Welfare Officer is only involved in a small number of cases, where s/he can offer counselling to the parents and children. Some parents are able to make good arrangements themselves; many cannot if children and money are the only weapons left with which to continue hostilities. Arrangements which look good on paper may break down in practice. Conciliation services are only available in a few areas – these services are offered by probation officers, marriage guidance councillors, social workers and others to enable divorcing couples to make the best possible arrangements between themselves and for the children.[9]

Our interest in divorce and the child's point of view was also prompted by personal experiences of divorce. We had been closely involved in a variety of post-divorce arrangements for children, ranging from bitterly contested custody to amicable and flexible access. We have been able to observe at close range the reactions of the children, though in our own case the observations may have been biased. Some of what we saw gave us cause for concern and motivated us to explore children's reactions.

In selecting material for this book it seemed neither possible nor desirable to present one hundred biographies. We were impressed by similar responses to similar circumstances and it is these that enabled us to arrive at four different 'profiles': children who described the long-lasting consequences of divorces as negative, positive, mixed and those who did not think they had been significantly affected. These 'profiles' were found to be linked to communication about divorce, post-divorce relationships with parents and the child's satisfaction with custody and access arrangements.

The first three chapters describe our method, the theoretical assumptions which guided us throughout and age-related differences. The chapters which follow reflect the format of our interviews and the main areas explored: memories of the pre-divorced family, how children learned about divorce and immediate reactions to the news; that which was helpful; custody and access arrangements; financial consequences; parental remarriage and relationships. Long-lasting consequences form the basis of our profiles. Our conclusions summarize briefly our findings and compare them with those of others. Finally we make some recommendations about who can help and how, addressing these to various groups.

Our case material has been chosen not at random, but to illustrate common themes as well as the great diversity of divorce-related experience. All identifying details have been disguised, without sacrificing accuracy. The opinions expressed throughout the book are those of the informants, with the exception of those expressed in the recommendations, which are ours. The aims of the study were simply to discover what children of divorced parents have to say about their own situation and to analyse this information for significant connections between experiences and self-perceived consequences. The aims of the book are to convey our findings and to make some recommendations about helping children to cope with the changes in their lives which follow divorce. The recommendations are addressed to parents, teachers, nurses, social workers and those involved in making laws and implementing them. All these people are involved in the process of divorce either personally or professionally.

## Notes and suggested reading

1. Central Statistical Office, Social Trends 1982, HMSO. Tables 2.13, 2.15, 2.16.
2. Kellmer Pringle M. (1980) *The Needs of Children.* Burnett Books Ltd. in association with André Deutsch Ltd.

   Dr Mia Kellmer Pringle, Director of the National Children's Bureau, has suggested that there should be two kinds of marriage contract: one for childless couples who should be allowed to divorce at will and another for couples with children under sixteen. For couples who are bringing up children the marriage contract should be more binding, encouraging them to put the interests of their children before their own.

The assumption behind this suggestion is that successful parenting needs to be shared by two parents, who should stay together at almost any cost.

3.  Rutter, M. 'Parent Child Separation: Psychological Effects on Children'. *Journal of Child Psychology and Psychiatry*, 12, 1971, 233–260.

> Professor M. Rutter, a well-known child psychiatrist, suggests that children from unhappy homes whose parents live together are in many respects worse off than children from homes broken by separation.

Professor Rutter suggests that:

> For the most part, the child is adversely affected by the tension and disharmony; the break-up of the family is only a minor influence.

4.  Goldstein, J., Freud, A. and Solnit, J. (1973): *Beyond the Best Interests of the Child*, Free Press.

> The authors, all experts in the field of child psychology and child care, suggest that the course which is least detrimental to the child should be chosen. A happy, intact, family serves 'the best interests of the child'. Since the law cannot legislate for human relationships, but can only make decisions about custody and access, the custodial parent should be the parent with whom the child has had the more continuous and better relationship – the child's psychological parent. It should be left totally to the custodial parent to determine what access is given to the other parent. Their reasons are: ... a 'visiting' or 'visited' parent has little chance to serve as a true object of love, trust and identification since this role is based on his being available on an uninterrupted day-to-day basis,

and

> Children have difficulty in relating positively to, profiting from and maintaining the contact with two psychological parents who are not in positive contact with each other. Loyalty conflicts ... may have devastating consequences by destroying the child's positive relationships to both parents. Thus we are led to conclude that in many cases it is best for the child to lose all contact with the non-custodial parent.

5.  Wallerstein, J. S. and Kelly, J. B. (1980): *Surviving the Breakup*. Grant McIntyre. New York: Basic Books, 1982. In *Surviving the Breakup*, based on an American study of divorced families, the authors advocate that:

> ... where possible, divorcing parents should be encouraged and helped to shape the post-divorce arrangements which permit and foster continuity in the children's relations with both parents.

> Only in exceptional circumstances should there be little or no contact between the child and the non-custodial parent.

6.  Tolstoy, Leo, *Anna Karenina*.
7.  Corman, A. (1979) *Kramer* v. *Kramer*. London: Collins, Sons & Co Ltd.

**8.** The following are some of the pioneering and recent studies of divorce and one-parent families:

Goode, Wm. (1969): *Women in Divorce*. New York: Free Press. (A pioneering study of divorced mothers).

Marsden, D. (1969): *Mothers Alone*. London: Allen Lane. (Based on a sample of lone mothers in receipt of social security).

George, V., and Wilding, P., (1972) *Motherless Families*. London: Routledge and Kegan Paul. (An inquiry into how lone fathers cope with bringing up children).

Hunt, M. (1968): *The World of the Formerly Married*. London: Allen Lane. (A vivid account of post-divorce reactions by an American journalist).

Weiss, R. (1975) *Marital Separation*. New York: Basic Books. (A sociological analysis of divorce and post-divorce adjustment).

Hart, N. (1976): *When Marriage Ends*. London: Tavistock Publications. (A study of divorce as a status passage, based on interviews and participant observation among members of a club for divorced and separated people).

**9.** Wilkinson, M. (1981): *Children and Divorce*. Oxford: Basil Blackwell. (An up-to-date review of the law relating to divorce; options which are open to judges and parents regarding arrangements for children and analysis of the role of probation and after-care service and social services departments in relation to the courts, divorcing parents and their children.

# CHAPTER 1

# ONE HUNDRED CHILDREN

'Alice sighed wearily. "I think you might do something better with the time"
she said, "than waste it asking riddles with no answers".'
(Lewis Carroll, *Alice's Adventures in Wonderland*)

Research is about asking questions, finding some answers as well as more
questions. It is a way of challenging firmly held beliefs based on
preconceived ideas and of new territories. The journey can be both exciting
and frustrating. Much research into human relationships and experiences –
as was ours – is motivated by the personal concerns of the researchers. It is
therefore even more important here than in other kinds of research to guard
against personal bias and to ensure that the conclusions reflect the opinions
of the participants and not just those of the researchers. It would, however,
be dishonest to disclaim all personal bias. Even computers have to be fed by
humans and can only analyse the information they are given. It is important
to find a way of gathering and analysing information which ensures the least
biased conclusions.

Our study was based on interviews with one hundred children, young
people and adults who agreed to talk to us about parental divorce, and in this
chapter we introduce them to the reader. What they had in common was the
breakup of their families before their eighteenth birthdays. In all other
respects the group was a mixed one, and we describe some of the varied
characteristics of the participants, such as their age at the time of the
interview and at parental separation, position in the family, sex, social class
and type of education. We explain how and where we found our volunteers,
the nature of our encounters and what we finally did with the wealth of
information gathered.

We set off on our journey of discovery equipped with much enthusiasm
and many ideas about what we wanted to find out. It was the spring of 1978.
We had no money and little spare time in which to accomplish what we
intended. We also had some doubts. Like the Mad Hatter, would we be
asking riddles to which there were no answers? The questions which were

uppermost in our minds were numerous. How do children find out that their parents are splitting up? What do they want to know? What are their reactions? What are some of the consequences? Are children harmed by the separation itself? How can they be helped to cope with such a major disruption in their lives?

Our doubts were reinforced by some funding bodies who did not share our enthusiasm and expressed concern about the possibility of our interviews having an upsetting effect on young children. We turned for reassurance to our professional experience in the course of which we have worked with many different kinds of family, including children of all ages. We had met many youngsters who, at the age of four, were excellent family diagnosticians and were able to sum up family relationships in a sentence or two. "Mum and Dad never agree, my sister always gets her own way and they don't take much notice when I say things" (Diane aged four). Children like talking to adults who take them seriously and try to enter their world, which for a young child is different from that of an older child, an adolescent or an adult. Children find relief in sharing painful feelings provided they do so at their own pace and are encouraged but not pressured to do so. When children feel guilty and uncomfortable talking about their families it is usually because they have picked up from adults internalized fear and guilt generated by closely guarded secrets and taboo subjects. Most families have their secrets and so have individuals. Unhappy people and unhappy families have more than their share. This is not to imply that all should always be revealed. We all have a secret corner that is our own and where we can hide when we need to.

Our enthusiasm was shared by many friends and colleagues and also our employing institution, the Polytechnic of North London, which agreed to provide funds and employed a full-time research assistant, a graduate in psychology with a teaching qualification. Our colleagues offered helpful advice. One of them, a statistician, converted a mass of detailed information into shared experience which eventually formed the basis of our conclusions. It was nice to know that those who knew us did not regard us as three weird sisters from *Macbeth* sworn to frightening little children.

Support and enthusiasm meant a great deal, but we also needed to make decisions about our method of gathering information: the size of our sample, who was to be included and what form the interviews would take. We also had to decide what was to be done with all the information thus obtained.

Our final decision was to interview in depth one hundred volunteers whose parents separated before the child's eighteenth birthday. We, and the children themselves, considered the separation rather than the actual divorce to have disrupted their lives. It was separation, not divorce, which was remembered. Some children did not even know what divorce meant at the time when it happened. "My mum and dad were divorced twice," we were told by one child, "once when Dad left and then when they went to court." What she remembered were her feelings of despair when her father left home. She did not remember the day on which her parents were legally divorced. This of course would not be true of all children. Some would remember both events, although not as equally significant. To ensure that the separation was permanent we chose to include only those whose parents had lived apart for two years. All but a few were also legally divorced.

All the volunteers, or their parents, lived, worked or studied in the Greater London area though many were born elsewhere. Fifty volunteers were to be under eighteen and fifty over eighteen. A sample of one hundred in a limited geographical area fitted in with the constraints of our financial resources yet was large enough to allow for some generalizations. We hoped it would allow for some comparisons between volunteers of different ages and from different social backgrounds.

We met our volunteers in a variety of ways. One of us had been involved in running a club for unattached people, the majority of whom had been divorced. All members of the club who had children were sent a letter describing our project and asking anyone who was interested to get in touch with us. A similar letter was sent to several branches of a self-help group for lone parents. Staff and students of an educational establishment were acquainted with the project through meetings and posters which were displayed in the building. Advertisements were inserted in the local press and some professional journals. We were also mentioned in bulletins of organizations concerned with divorced and separated people. We were unable to obtain permission to approach children in local authority children's homes.

Our volunteers came in the following ways:

| Source of contact | Number |
| --- | --- |
| Local press | 36 |
| Educational establishment | 29 |
| Others | 16 |
| Club | 12 |
| Self-help group | 5 |
| Professional journals | 2 |
| Total | 100 |

'Others' were mainly those who found out about the project from volunteers already participating.

The volunteers came from sixty-seven families. Forty-five were the only member of their family who was interviewed. Fifty-five belonged to twenty-two families in which more than one member offered to take part.

The youngest participant was six, the oldest fifty-seven. The age-groups were represented as follows:

| Age at the time of interview | Number |
| --- | --- |
| 11 and under | 15 |
| 12 and under 18 | 35 |
| 18 and under 25 | 23 |
| Over 25 | 27 |
| Total | 100 |

At the time of parental separation most children were between five and twelve.

| Age at separation | Number |
| --- | --- |
| 4 and under | 20 |
| 5 and under 12 | 60 |
| 12 and under 18 | 20 |
| Total | 100 |

Some were only children, others had brothers and sisters.

| Position in family | Number |
| --- | --- |
| Youngest | 37 |
| Middle | 16 |
| Eldest | 33 |
| Only child | 14 |
| Total | 100 |

Many more females than males offered to participate: sixty-five girls and women and thirty-five boys and men. This is not suprising. It is women rather than men who are expected to show their feelings and to look after the emotional needs of others within and outside the family. This makes it harder for men to talk about personal relationships. Women talk about such matters more fully and readily, maybe because they are expected to do so and have such an expectation of themselves.

The volunteers came from a wide range of social backgrounds. Some had fathers who were professional men or had their own business. Others had clerical jobs and some were unskilled labourers. Mothers' occupations ranged from clerical to domestic. Many mothers had not worked before separation and returned to work or full-time studies after the breakup of the marriage.

To determine social class we used the Registrar General classification.[1]

| Class of chief wage-earner in the family at the time of separation | Number |
|---|---|
| I | 15 |
| II | 41 |
| III non-manual | 18 |
| III manual | 10 |
| IV | 8 |
| V | 6 |
| Not known | 2 |
| Total | 100 |

We also asked those over 18 about their own occupation. Married women were classified according to theirs. A high number were students, others were mainly in clerical, selling and nursing jobs.

Social class of those over 18 is given below (the Registrar General classification was used).

| | |
|---|---|
| I | 1 |
| II | 15 |
| III non-manual | 10 |
| III manual | 00 |
| IV | 3 |
| Students | 18 |
| Housewives | 3 |
| Total | 50 |

✶

We were also interested in the type of education the child was still having or had completed. Eleven children were still attending primary school. Of the rest 33 had had or were undergoing further or higher education, 59 had attended comprehensive school, 30 had attended a grammar school. Many children had received more than one type of education, for example, those who been at both a comprehensive and a boarding-school. A high number of children (16) were sent to boarding-school, following the separation of the parents.

There are many ways of collecting information. Interviews, postal questionnaires and participant observation are some of them. For the purpose of our research we decided on depth interviews. An interview, like a photograph, captures mood and expression at a particular time as well as what belongs to the past. The past is filtered through each person's current situation. We were surprised to find how vivid some memories were. Age and time-distance seemed unimportant. We were amazed how much of the past could be compressed into an hour or so and shared with a stranger. Some people find it easier to talk to strangers than to members of their own family. There is no fear of upsetting anyone. We were told by some participants and parents that following the interview for the first time they were able to talk to each other about things concerning divorce which had never been discussed before.

Most interviews were carried out in the volunteer's home, though a few adolescents chose to come to us, to ensure privacy. In the case of all those who were under 18 we obtained parental consent as well as their own. Our contacts with parents were limited to explaining, as we did to everyone, that we were collecting information from children of separated parents and hoping to write a book based on it. We admired the parents' willingness to be excluded. One father did admit his intention to hide a tape-recorder in the room, but then changed his mind. We were grateful for hospitality, for the way in which we were received and welcomed.

All the interviews were conducted by three people: the authors and our research assistant. All but a few were tape-recorded and all fully written up. It is not possible to eliminate altogether personal bias in this kind of interview. However, we listened to each other's tapes to ensure that we were asking questions in a similar way and not trying to prompt the answers.

Our aim was to gather information, not to provide counselling. Three of our volunteers felt they needed help with problems related to divorce. We suggested where they could get it. Most of our volunteers seemed to be motivated by the desire to help others, albeit indirectly. For many this was the first time they had been listened to and they were glad to have the opportunity to share their feelings with someone else. 'This is the first time I have ever talked to any one like this,' was a typical comment. There were also those who had talked to their parents, relatives and friends and a few had talked to professional helpers such as social workers.

Some had suffered a great deal and had very painful memories, others considered themselves lucky that divorce had not made much difference to their lives. Some parents thought that their child had been badly affected while others did not. While chatting to us before we saw the child some said that their relationship with the child was good while others, particularly parents of adolescent children, referred to difficulties between them and their sons and daughters. We spoke to parents who felt very bitter towards their ex-spouse and those who were 'better friends than when we were married'. The reasons given for offering to participate did not seem to be biased in any particular way beyond a wish to share with us both good and bad experiences so that they could be passed on for the benefit of others in similar circumstances.

This letter was typical of many that we received:

Dear Sheila Burns and Yvette Walczak
I am 14 years old, I have a brother and sister of 16 and 17 years old. My parents have been divorced for 8 years and I live with my mother.
I saw your article [advertisement] in the Hendon times about the project and I would be interested in helping. My mother has agreed to my participating in the project.

Yours sincerely,
Nigel Smith
I agree to let my son take part in the project.
Joan Smith.

Our interviews were as informal as possible, but there was also a structure provided by the use of a questionnaire which was memorized by each interviewer. The questionnaire is reproduced in the Appendix. At the beginning we were helped with the selection and wording of the questions by a dozen or so volunteers, including some children aged seven and eight who made extremely helpful comments. Thus we found that the question 'Where were you born?' often prompted the answer, 'at home', or 'in hospital', rather than the country of origin. Similar questions, we found, could be asked regardless of age though the wording had to vary. Whereas adults would be asked directly about their parents' marriage, a young child was more likely to respond to 'how did your mum and dad get on when they were still living in the same house?'

What we wanted to find out and what the volunteers seemed to want to talk about mostly coincided. There were a number of themes which were common concerns, including separation, loss of one parent, access arrangements, sources of help, financial consequences, parental remarriage and the long-term consequences of separation.

Some consequences were considered to be transient, others long-lasting. Two years after separation (for some much longer) there were those who considered themselves to have been badly affected, while others were not at all affected. Some mentioned only positive consequences. There was also a group who saw the consequences as mixed – some good and some bad.

The information gathered in the course of our interviews was transcribed on to coded sheets which could be analysed to show which comments and responses were made with some regularity. Those made by five or more people were taken into account in analysing the data. Computer-produced tables showed the frequency with which certain responses and comments occurred and connections between various events surrounding separation and longer term 'outcomes'. A test was applied (chi-square) to ensure that such connections were significant and to eliminate those that could have occurred purely by chance.

We cannot claim that those who participated in the project represent all children of divorced parents. A fully representative sample would have required an enormous expenditure of time and money. At the same time, because so many responses were shared by those from different backgrounds, and in many respects our findings are similar to those of a major American study,[2] we believe that much can be learned from our conversations with those who so willingly confided in us.

# Notes

1. Social class   I   Professional occupations
                  II   intermediate occupations including most managerial and administrative
                  III   non-manual (e.g. clerical)
                  III   manual
                  IV   semi-skilled
                  V   unskilled
2. Wallerstein, Judith S., and Kelly, J. B. (1980): *Surviving the Breakup*, London. Grant McIntyre.

# CHAPTER 2

# THEORETICAL GUIDELINES

"Many of the most intense of all human emotions arise during the formation, the maintenance, the disruption and the renewal of affectional bonds."
Bowlby, J. *The Making and Breaking of Affectional Bonds.*

The aim of our study has been to collect and analyse information about children's reactions to parental separation. During this process we were guided and informed by a number of theories relating to child development. What follows is an attempt to summarize these and suggest selected reading.

## Individual differences

Our study has tended to explore and highlight common divorce-related reactions rather than individual differences, while being aware that such differences exist and have been described in the literature on child development.

Infants differ in their sucking and sleeping rhythms and their excitability and responsiveness to stimuli. Children differ according to physical characteristics, strength of instinctual drives, nature and intensity of attachments, intellectual functioning, interests, aptitudes and vulnerability to stress. The child's parents and others respond to the child's characteristics as well as influence the child by their own. Thus a pattern of interaction is set up from the moment of birth, or even before.

A variety of theoretical approaches address individual differences as well as processes and experiences shared by all children, adolescents and adults.

## Psychoanalytic theories

Psychoanalytic theories chart the course of emotional development and trace the pattern of adult mental life to the first five years, regarded as the formative period. Mental processes are both conscious and unconscious and it is the latter which are the main focus of psychoanalysis both as a theory of mental functioning and as therapy. The unconscious has several layers and it was Melanie Klein who postulated that greed and envy belong to the deepest strata. Whereas Freud evolved his theories through the analysis of adults, Melanie Klein did this through child analysis and the observation of infants and young children. Mental life is governed by the existence of two groups of instincts: the life and death instincts, both present from birth. The aim of mental activity is to maximize pleasure and avoid pain. Gratification can be achieved both in reality and fantasy.

The structure of personality is tripartite: the id, ego and super-ego. The id exists at birth. The origins of ego and super-ego are the object of some controversy within the psychoanalytic movement. The id is the seat of all primitive instincts. Its wishes are compelling and immediate. Contradictory feelings can exist side by side as the id is totally irrational. It is also omnipotent and wishes as well as actions are assumed to result in desired outcomes. Thus the id's omnipotence is seen as responsible for reparation and destruction, the latter causing feelings of guilt.

The ego mediates between the id, the demands of reality and the moral injunctions of the super-ego. The ego is partly unconscious and partly conscious. Its functions are: cognition, memory, synthesis, planning, mediation, defence mechanisms and object relations. Defence mechanisms include repression, denial, rationalization and projection. They are necessary to cope with anxiety, which is aroused by the instincts, events in the real world and prohibitions of the super-ego. The ego relates to objects (people and things in the environment) in a variety of ways. Objects are perceived partly as they are and also in terms of fantasy. They are endowed with characteristics belonging to the child and projected into them. The internal world is then made up of the child's instinctual life as well as of other people (objects) taken inside. The nature of internal objects determines the state of the internal world. Good internalized objects lead to a sense of well-being, trust in others and a positive self-image. Bad objects have the opposite effect.

The super-ego, like the ego, is partly conscious, partly unconscious. It is that part of personality which has internalized moral rules and standards of behaviour. It contains prohibitions and proscriptions. It is the source of guilt when its prohibitions have been violated.

Psychoanalytic theory charts the course of development in terms of sources of instinctual satisfaction and preoccupation with body zones. The first year is referred to as the oral stage. It is a time when the baby derives pleasure and satisfaction through sucking and biting. In the very early stages, the baby, according to Melanie Klein, relates to parts rather than whole objects, such as the breast rather than the whole mother. The second year is known as the anal stage due to the child's preoccupation with this zone. During this year toilet training takes place and the toddler derives satisfaction from both holding and giving up the faeces. The genital stage from three to five years of age is characterized by curiosity about the genital zone, which becomes the main source of pleasure. It is during this stage that Freud postulated the emergence of sexual feelings towards the parent of the opposite sex and rivalry and fear of punishment by the same-sexed parent. Strong incest taboos in most families prevent these feelings from emerging into consciousness and being acted out. The conflict is resolved by renouncing the parent of the opposite sex and identifying with the parent of the same sex, accompanied by internalization of sex-linked characteristics and moral standards. According to Melanie Klein, oedipal feelings emerge much earlier than as postulated by Freud. Whereas Freud emphasized that awareness of sexual differences leads to penis envy in girls, Melanie Klein suggested that both boys and girls envy the mother's ability to produce and feed babies.

The ages of five to ten are termed the latency stage. During this period instinctual drives are quiescent. The psychic energy is freed for learning and exploration. Children make great strides in their learning and social development, and appear self-possessed.

Puberty, beginning with the onset of menstruation in girls and seminal emission in boys, is a time when instinctual drives again dominate mental life. Many adolescents deal with their own and others' sexuality and the return of oedipal wishes by becoming acutely embarrassed by sexual feelings and denying their existence. This may account for the need to deny the sexuality of their parents and discomfort related to contact with the parent of the opposite sex as well as feelings of rivalry with the same-sex parent.

Theory relating to the instinctual life and development of the individual has been used (e.g., by Pincus and Dare) to explain certain family processes. Much of family life revolves around birth, death and sexual intercourse. Strong taboos prevent the acknowledgement and open discussion of important subjects. This leads to the formation of family secrets and myths which cast family members into inappropriate roles, necessary to perpetuate such myths as a defence against anxiety.

One of the family's tasks is to cater for the needs of the growing child, which are different at each stage of development. Unconscious processes play an important part in both marital and family interaction. Unresolved conflicts from the past are relived in marital and family scenes. The marital relationship acts as a container of powerful feelings and also offers the possibility of reliving and resolving past conflicts in a new relationship; it can also break down if powerful negative feelings from the past intervene in a destructive way. Family members are at the receiving end of each other's projections and also of feelings inappropriately transferred from the past.

## Attachment theory

Attachment theory has been evolved by Bowlby, who became interested in studying the effect on child development both of instincts and the environment. The theory has its roots in ethology – study of social and familial behaviour in birds and animals. Each species is equipped at birth with a species-specific behaviour repertoire. There are critical phases for developing each type of behaviour and they are evoked and extinguished by environmental stimuli and responses. What happens during the critical phases affects whether or not the response develops, the intensity with which it is inhibited, the motor form it takes and what particular stimuli activate and terminate it. Attachment behaviour is part of an infant's behavioural repertoire. Its aim is to maintain proximity to the mother to ensure survival. 'Mother' need not be the biological mother or even female; in his later writings Bowlby recognized the possibility of interchangeable family roles. The infant maintains proximity through a number of types of behaviour: crying, smiling, clinging, following. These are terminated by an appropriate response from the mother. Intensely ambivalent feelings of love and hate accompany attachment behaviour while love and security help to resolve ambivalence and create trust in the environment. Attachment is at its most intense during the fourth quarter of the first year and continues with some intensity during the second and third year. After this children are able to tolerate brief separations. Attachment behaviour is intensified in situations which evoke fear and unhappiness: illness, darkness, strange surroundings. Securely attached children, whose needs have been met, are able to tolerate separation and explore their environment more readily than insecurely attached ones. Bowlby postulated a tendency towards mono-tropy – most children become attached to single mother-figures.

Bowlby discovered a number of common reactions which follow disruption of an attachment bond due to separation. He identified three phases: protest, despair and detachment. Separation, he believed, could have harmful effects on mental health both in the short and long run.

Bowlby's ideas have been the source of some controversy. What has mainly been questioned is the tendency to monotropy, whether 'mother' needs to be female, and the lasting consequences of separation. 'Maternal deprivation' has been said to be an imprecise concept. Nevertheless there is fairly general agreement that the development of a bond with one or more persons who provide love and security is essential for healthy development. Its disruption causes mental pain and anger. The need for bonding or preference which one individual has for another continues in adult life. In Bowlby's own words 'Many of the most intense of all human emotions arise during the formation, the maintenance, the disruption and the renewal of affectional bonds.' Loss of important figures in adult life through death or other circumstances such as divorce is followed by a number of clearly distinguishable reactions and stages: numbness and shock on initial impact; searching and pining; disorganization and despair; some degree of reorganization. Pathological reactions to loss include initial denial, prolonged grieving, inability to give up the lost person and reorganize one's life without them.

There has been little research on the effects of the disruption of attachment bonds, where the main attachment is to the father or both parents equally. However, there is no reason to believe that if the nature of the attachment is similar to the mother-child bond, the consequences of disruption would be different from those which Bowlby described.

## Cognitive development

Piaget, a Swiss psychologist, laid down the foundations of understanding the child's intellectual development. Like all psychological theories, his have also been the subject of controversy including criticism of methodology. Nevertheless his guidelines are widely accepted. Piaget is known as a genetic epistemologist, having investigated the relationship between the nature and origin of knowledge and human development. Certain cognitive processes – structural invariants – are universal and independent of age, the main ones being accommodation, assimilation and organization. All individuals have to accommodate to objects in their enviroment. In turn these objects and their characteristics become incorporated into already existing mental structures. This proceeds through various stages: at first repetitive action towards an object helps the infant to remember it; the next step is differentiating between objects; these are the beginning of thinking about the world. Having learned to recognize differences, the child learns about similarities. Finally an object is recognized by bringing together a variety of cognitive structures such as vision and touch.

Cognitive acts are governed by planned sequences known as schemas which lead to a desired result through a sequence of actions. The behaviour which results from the processes of accommodation, assimilation and organization is governed by mental structures, which vary with age. Four major structures have been identified: the period of sensori-motor intelligence (birth to two years); the period of preoperational thought (two to six years); the period of concrete operations (six to eleven years) and the period of formal operations (eleven to fifteen years). The baby's behaviour is reflex in nature. During the second period symbols can be substituted for the real objects. During the third stage objects can be grouped and symbolic thinking becomes well organized. It is only in adolescence that abstract thinking becomes possible. Hypotheses can be formulated and tested. Not only the present, but the future, can be contemplated.

A young child is "egocentric": only able to see the world from his or her point of view. She or he is unaware of other points of view and therefore cannot make comparisons. Egocentricity does not imply emotional selfishness, but an intellectual inability to see situations as others might see them.

## Systems theory

The systems theory was evolved by natural scientists. When applied to the family, the theory is an approach which sees it as being more than the sum of its parts. It defines the family as consisting of individual members, their personalities and characteristics and the relationships between them. It stresses the interdependence and interrelationhips within the family structure (as in the parental and parent/child sub-system), and looks at its interaction with suprasystems outside its boundaries such as neighbourhood and school.

Any change affecting an individual member or subsystem affects the whole family. The functioning of the system depends on communication between its members, which takes various forms ranging from being free and open to contradictory messages and metaphors which may not be easily understood by the members to whom they are addressed.

The theories which have been briefly outlined address different areas of individual development and familial relationships. They are in many ways complementary. For instance, a young child would be unable to form attachments to a particular person without being able to recognize and distinguish them from strangers. The child's intellectual egocentricity and omnipotent feelings largely account for a sense of guilt generated by destructive wishes. In the particular situation studied it was expected that reactions to divorce would be influenced by the child's cognitive capacity to understand events, the nature of his/her tie to the figure from whom the child became totally or partially separated and defence mechanisms habitually employed to cope with stress. The family systems approach brought with it an implicit assumption that the child as a member of his/her family is affected by familial relationships and happenings as well as the family's contacts with the outside world.

Some psychological theories, particularly the psychoanalytic, stress that psychological damage in early life cannot be easily, if ever, repaired. Recently there has been more stress on the value of reparative experience, notably on the basis of evidence collected by Clarke and Clarke, whose ideas inspired us to investigate ways in which damage associated with parental divorce could be repaired.

## Notes and Suggested Reading

### General

Bee, H. L. and Mitchell, S. K. (1980): *The Developing Person*. London: Harper and Row.

Clarke, A. M. and Clarke, A. D. B. (1976): *Early Experience, Myth and Evidence*. London: Open Books.

Richards, M. (1976): *The Integration of a Child into a Social World*. Cambridge University Press, 3rd ed.

### Individual differences

Kellmer Pringle, M. (1982): *The Needs of Children*. London: Hutchinson, 4th ed.
Richards, M. (1980): *Infancy*. London: Harper and Row.

### Psychoanalytic Theories

Freud, S. (1953–1964): *The Complete Psychological Works*, London: Hogarth Press.
Hall, C. S. (1954): *A Primer of Freudian Psychology*. New York: New American Library.
Klein, M. and others (1952): *Developments in Psychoanalysis*. Ed. Joan Riviere, London: Hogarth Press.
Klein, M. (1975): *The Writings of Melanie Klein*, Vols. I–IV. London: Hogarth Press.

Pincus, L. and Dare, C. (1978): *Secrets in the Family*. London: Faber and Faber.

Segal, H. (1979): *Klein*. London: Fontana/Collins.

## Cognitive Development

Beard, R. M. (1969): *An Outline of Piaget's Developmental Psychology*. London: Routledge and Kegan Paul.

Piaget, J. (1953): *The Origins of Intelligence in the Child*. London: Routledge and Kegan Paul.

## Attachment Theory

Bowlby, J. (1969): *Attachment and Loss*. Vol 1. *Attachment*, London: Hogarth Press.

Bowlby, J. (1973): Vol 2: *Separation: Anxiety and Anger*. London: Hogarth Press.

Bowlby, J. (1979): Vol 3: *Loss*. London: Hogarth Press.

Bowlby, J. (1980): *The Making and Breaking of Affectional Bonds*. London: Tavistock Publications.

Rutter, M. (1972): *Maternal Deprivation Reassessed*. Harmondsworth, Penguin Books.

## Systems Theory

Barker, P. (1981): *Basic Family Therapy*. London: Granada.

Hall, A. D. and Fagan, R. E. (1965): "Definition of System, in General Systems": *Yearbooks of the Society for the Advancement of General Systems Theory*. Ed. L. von Bertalanffy and Rapoport, A.

Walrond–Skinner, S. (1976): *Family Therapy: The Treatment of Natural Systems*. London: Routledge and Kegan Paul.

# CHAPTER 3

# THE RHUBARB PATCH; TALKING ABOUT DIVORCE WITH CHILDREN, ADOLESCENTS AND ADULTS

'I would like my parents to break up being divorced... I feel Daddy won't ever come back, but he will, he might come back.' (Charles, aged six).

"I miss my father, sometimes I feel sad but only when I am very tired or very bored... I am happy most of the time... we send each other funny postcards." (Sarah, aged ten).

"I hate my father... my mother should have chucked him out much sooner instead of suggesting Marriage Guidance... when he comes I go upstairs." (Debbie, aged fourteen).

"As I sat crying in the rhubarb patch at the bottom of our garden many thoughts flashed through my mind... my father had just said his usual good-byes after one of his weekends with us but this time I knew he would not be coming back... now all I can feel for him is compassion." (David, aged twenty-one).

"My father was the original beatnik, born before his time, my mother was a highly conventional woman. They were incompatible." (Marion, aged thirty-seven).

These comments about absent fathers were made by those who were at different stages of life. We chose them to introduce this chapter, which is on talking about divorce to children, young people and adults of different ages. Elsewhere we emphasize the similarities between responses to similar experiences; this chapter is about differences, specifically related to age, between those in similar circumstances: those whose parents stopped being a couple.

For the purpose of comparison and to highlight the differences we divided those who took part in the study into four age groups: children aged six to eleven, adolescents aged twelve to seventeen, young adults aged eighteen to twenty-four and older adults aged twenty-five and over. Such broad groupings were partly dictated by the size of the sample and partly by the age-differences which seemed particularly significant. To guide us in our understanding of age-related differences we assumed a developmental framework: the child is a developing person, physically, intellectually, emotionally and socially. We looked for differences in these four areas in so far as they were applicable to the process of divorce. We assumed that when physical growth stops the young person continues to mature and that in adulthood the repertoire of skills, knowledge, and ways of responding and coping with life continue to expand indefinitely.[1]

The world in which we live is also in the process of constant change. In the last twenty years or so attitudes and laws relating to divorce have changed. There are many more divorced families than there were and therefore children whose parents divorced recently are likely to know more children in a similar situation than those whose parents divorced many years ago. It is no longer necessary to prove that one parent was guilty and the other innocent. It is no longer necessary to feel ashamed and hide the fact that one's parents are divorced, since attitudes are now more permissive and accepting of divorce. What we tried to find out was how changes in legislation and attitudes were translated into individual experience and at what age they made a difference to how individuals perceived themselves and their circumstances.

We have chosen two children, Charles and Sarah, to represent the youngest age group since the younger the child the faster the rate at which changes take place in all areas of development, and there were many noticeable differences between the youngest and the older children. Debbie represents the adolescent age group, David and Marion younger and older adults respectively.

## Children aged six to eleven

### Charles

The interviewer was introduced to Charles by his mother and his sister, both of whom indicated that Charles had been apprehensive about meeting the interviewer, but nevertheless seemed very keen to talk to her about divorce. Charles, at the age of six, was the youngest of all the children who took part in our study. He is a bright cheerful boy. When the interviewer arrived at his house Charles, his mother and his sister sat together round a table. The mother had welcomed the interviewer and for a short time they talked together before the children joined in the conversation, and began to discuss the party they were to attend that evening. The interviewer was able to reveal some information about herself such as where she worked, where she lived and the names of her children. She heard about some of the exploits of the family's cat and told them about hers.

At the beginning of the interview, Charles and the interviewer played for a while with the tape-recorder, practising speaking into it, playing it back to hear what had been said and how it sounded and laughing at themselves. The interviewer explained that even though Charles had agreed to talk to her he still did not have to answer all the questions. If there were questions he disliked or could not answer he should say so. When Charles was ready, the interviewer began with Charles holding the microphone as he said he had seen in television interviews. Being in charge of the microphone seemed important to Charles and he certainly spoke into it with confidence. It seemed important too that the interview was started with simple, direct questions to which he knew the answers: his name, his age, the name of his school and who lived with him.

Charles said he was too young to remember the time when his mummy and daddy lived together but his mother has spoken to him of this time and he thought that for them it was happy. He did not know why his parents decided to live separately, but thought it might be because one of them wanted to live in town and the other one in the country. They liked different places.

Charles no longer sees his father and cannot remember him very well. He does not even know when he last saw him. He is not sure why his father stopped coming and said sadly, "It was probably 'cos he does not like us anymore."

Charles would like to see his father and would like him to come back. He would like his parents to "break up being divorced." His father has married again. Charles has not met the new wife and does not know anything about her. He knows that his father sends money to his mother, but not to him. He does not see the connection between this money and himself. "It is money for her." Charles has told his mother that he would like to see his father and she said that Charles could telephone him. Charles knows how to use the telephone, but seemed reluctant to telephone his father to whom he has not spoken for some time.

Charles talked about things he and his mother do together and said that he loved her very much and she also loves him. He also likes his mother's boyfriend and referred to him as "a very nice friend of mine". Asked if his mummy and her boyfriend might marry, Charles was not sure. In reply to whether he would like it Charles said: "Yes-no." "Yes", he explained, meant they might stay together, "no" meant they might split up.

Charles ended the interview by saying that he wanted his father to come back and stay "all five of us". This number included mother's boyfriend, mother, Charles, his sister and father, but not father's new wife, whom Charles has not met. "I feel Daddy won't ever come back, but he will, I feel that he will, he might come back."

The youngest children, aged six and seven, had some difficulty in comprehending what was happening and seemed bewildered by a number of things. They could not always understand why their parents had to live apart and that the separation was permanent. Their thinking was concrete. They could understand that they were living with only one parent and that the other one was somewhere else. Divorce, remarriage and maintenance are abstract ideas and their connotations are hard for a young child to grasp. Divorce and remarriage do not imply a permanent state of affairs, especially if this is not to the child's liking. A new wife or husband does not mean much to a young child unless he or she is a concrete person whom the child has met and with whom he has had some contact. Maintenance is an abstract concept which is quite meaningless. It is 'money' which is seen as having some value and if it is actually given to a parent for the child's maintenance it is not seen as being directly for the child, but regarded as belonging to the parent.

Young children are egocentric. This does not imply selfishness, but rather the inability to see things from another person's perspective. Children who would like to have a parent back to live with them can only see this from their point of view; they cannot envisage a situation in which a new wife and an ex-wife live under the same roof. Parents are seen as belonging to the child and children have only very vague notions as to how the parents relate to each other. These notions are usually based on what the child is told. When parents argue or fight, this impinges on the child directly and he is aware of his feelings rather than those of the parents. A child is the centre of his world. He believes that whatever happens may have been caused by him. When a parent stops visiting the child does not see that the parent may have other commitments or may not wish to have any contact with his ex-spouse. It is the child who feels no longer loved or worthy of love and who feels that he may in some way have caused the rejection.

Young children find it hard to formulate their own opinions and tend to model themselves on those on whom they are most dependent and with whom they have most interaction. What they say and feel about a parent with whom they have little contact may echo the sentiments of the closest to them. Thus many children in the younger age range repeated the opinion of one of their parents, presenting it as their own.

We were impressed by the willingness of young children to talk to us. Of course their vocabularies are limited and this meant that the meaning of words sometimes had to be explained. Once words such as separation and access were explained children were able to grasp their meaning. Children had some difficulty in describing their feelings in detail and differentiating between shades of sadness or anger. They demonstrated their feelings by actions and facial expressions, by crying or looking puzzled, and needed help with putting things into words.

Sadness, anger, fear, relief, and other emotions are not confined to any particular age. Similar feelings are shared by the very young, the very old and by all those in between. What is special about younger children is that they find it hard to comprehend the reason for their feelings and may be quite overwhelmed by them. Some of the children seemed to feel an enduring sadness, both at home and at school. Children have fewer ways of coping with feelings than do adolescents and adults.

One way a young child can cope with feelings is to believe that wishes can come true. If a child wishes his parents to come back then he believes that this may have the desired result. If a young child wants to find a lost parent he may decide to look for him but we were told by some children that they only got as far as the front gate and no one ever knew of their intention. The world of young children is one of part reality and part magic. Rational solutions cannot be easily found without help from a sympathetic adult such as a parent who helps a child to write a postcard or use the telephone, or who shows photographs of the absent parent or makes it quite clear that some of the money received as maintenance is for the child's pocket-money.

When talking to young children we become very aware of how dependent they are on those with whom they live. This is usually the parent, very occasionally a grandparent and in the case of those whose parents remarried, the step-parent. These people were most frequently mentioned by young children. Friends were seen by the children as playmates, not as confidants and potential helpers. Young children did not seem to compare themselves with other children and if they knew other divorced families they did not mention this as being important to them, as did children aged eight and over. The world outside the home environment is still filtered to the child through the family. Because there were no alternatives available, what was happening at home was very important.

## Sarah

Sarah is a lively and intelligent girl who was in her last year of primary school when we met her. She lives with her mother and younger brother in a house in which she has lived as long as she can remember. When the interviewer arrived Sarah firmly took charge of the situation by ushering her three-year-old brother out of the room, meeting with some resistance as he seemed rather keen to play with the tape recorder. Sarah firmly shut the door behind him with the injunction to "stay with Mummy in the kitchen".

Sarah said that her parents separated when she was seven. Her mother is a nurse who has returned to full-time studies, and Sarah seemed somewhat amused by this and quite proud of her mother. She was not sure of her father's occupation but thought it was something important as "he sometimes goes to work by aeroplane". Sarah's memories of her infant school years and before are patchy and mostly happy. She could remember things which happened when she was three, such as going to see the film *Bambi* on her third birthday. She remembers outings with her parents. She also described in some detail an exciting holiday the family had in America while her mother was expecting her second child. Sarah liked the weather and would not mind living abroad all the time.

"I love my Daddy very much, I love both my parents very much," said Sarah with strong conviction. She remembers her father laughing and joking with her. "I like jokey people." Her mother also laughs and jokes with Sarah. She feels she can talk to her parents about anything.

After the family returned from their holiday in America, Sarah remembers that things were not as happy as before. There were arguments. Pointing to a door, Sarah recalled an occasion when "Daddy made Mummy so angry that she kicked the door and there was a large dent." There was another vividly remembered quarrel when Sarah's baby brother fell off a table. "Daddy got very angry and Mummy was crying and she kept pulling me away from Daddy and in the end they were both crying." Sarah remembers feeling upset and frightened. She thinks that her parents split up because in the end they were having too many arguments. This is what she has been told by both of them on many different occasions. Sarah feels that both parents separately told her all that she wants to know, but if she wanted to know more she could ask them.

Sarah remembers feeling very unhappy and crying when her father moved out. She used to see him frequently, but since he went to live abroad she can only see him during school holidays and she looks forward to these. She knows that her mother is willing to let her stay with her father. Between the times when they see each other Sarah and her father write letters and postcards and send photographs. Occasionally they speak on the telephone. Sarah could not choose the parent with whom she lived as her father travels a great deal and so living with him would not have been practicable. She still misses her father, but feels sad only when she is tired or very bored. Most of the time she feels happy.

Sarah's father has a girlfriend whom Sarah likes. She does not think her father would have chosen anyone "horrible" but, if he had, Sarah would not have been pleased. She also likes the girlfriend's parrot which she thinks is very clever. Mother's boyfriend visits and sometimes stays the night. Sarah was quite emphatic that her mother did not love him. Sarah likes him but not as much as she liked her mother's previous boyfriend who was tall and handsome and spent time playing with Sarah. She would have been pleased if her mother had married him and was disappointed when they parted company.

If there has been any change in the family's financial circumstances Sarah has not noticed it. She is satisfied with the amount of pocket-money she receives. Her mother does not discuss money matters with Sarah, who pays for sweets and trips to the cinema. Her mother provides everything else.

Sarah likes school and has many friends. Having divorced parents is quite common these days, she thinks. "In my class there are groups, you know, and in my group there is Lucy. Her parents are separated. And there is Jessica. Her mother and father are also separated. This only leaves Jean and Claire. Their parents are still together." Sarah does not think that having divorced parents has had an effect on her. She has got used to the idea and there are other children to keep her company. She gets on well with both her parents and knows that they love her. She thinks that her father may love her more than he loves her brother since he knows her better and they spent more time together before her parents lived apart.

The older children in the youngest age group, those aged eight, nine, ten and eleven, differed in many respects from the younger ones. They had achieved far greater understanding of their situation and were able to seek more rational solutions as well as being able to relate to a wider range of people. We were impressed with the reasoning powers of these children.

They were able to understand that their parents were not going to be reunited. They could give what they thought were the reasons for the separation and were able to think of both the advantages and disadvantages of their current situation. The children who, for instance, had a preference for living with one parent rather than the other gave reasons such as wanting to get to know a parent better or preferring the parent who did not try to influence them against the other.

Older children gave the impression of being capable of independent thinking, when they said they liked a parent, even though this opinion was not shared by the mother or father. This had its disadvantages as it often put children in a position of conflicting loyalties. Children who wanted to see a parent, but knew the visits were upsetting the other parent, were not sure what to do for the best. This also applied to children who preferred a different visiting arrangement to that chosen by the visiting parent. This independence of judgement also applied to step-parents and parents' other partners. Older children form their own views and are not as much influenced by parental preferences as the younger ones.

The older children aged eight to eleven expressed a whole range of feelings and gave the impression that somehow they were in charge of them. This fitted in with the stage of development when the children are relatively at peace with themselves and much of their energy is available for learning and exploration. They appeared to us composed and able to cope. They had acquired a wider vocabulary, and were able to differentiate between the finer shades of similar feelings. They were able to indicate whether they felt a little or very sad and in what circumstances and that feeling tired or bored or unwell brought on certain reactions.

The repertoire of 'coping' skills increases with age, experience, and the ability to think rationally. Older children were able to use the telephone, write letters, and visit parents without direct help, but still had great need for approval and emotional support. Time acquired new meaning. Older children were more able to wait and if they missed a parent whom they did not see often, they could count the weeks and months and look forward to the next visit.

The older children talked to us not only about the people they lived with, their immediate family and parents' partners staying or visiting, but they told us about school, teachers and friends. Their world had expanded and the number of important relationships had increased. When talking about parents they did so in a less self-centred way. They were able to be pleased when a parent was involved in some enjoyable activity, had friends, or belonged to a club. Some of the children spoke of worrying about a parent who appeared sad or cried. They expressed concern, but the remedy was not known. Older children described not only what they did with each parent, but also how they got on and what they felt about it. For instance we were told by children who were able to have conversations with their parents how much they appreciated it. They could discern when a parent was trying to influence them as, for instance, against the other parent.

School had become an important place, as had various people in it. We were told how the children were progressing, what subjects they enjoyed and which they did not, and what effect divorce had on their progress at school. Some teachers were singled out as being specially "nice" and understanding if the child was upset and needed comforting. Other teachers were seen as not very sympathetic or interested in the child.

Friends had become increasingly important. We were told about who the children played with and where, also who their best friends were and why they liked them. It was our impression that children did not talk to each other about divorce, but knowing other children at school who had divorced parents or perhaps because a parent belonged to a club for divorced and separated people was particularly important. It made the child feel that there was nothing different or special about its family. None of the children spoke about feeling ashamed or needing to conceal that they had divorced parents. It would seem that permissive attitudes to divorce influence how children feel about their situation.

## Adolescents, aged twelve to seventeen

### Debbie

Debbie is fourteen. She lives with her mother and younger brother. She also has an older brother who is married. Her parents separated when she was twelve. She has always got on well with her mother and two brothers, but not so well with her father. She related how she tried for years to get close to her father. She tried to talk to him and be close to him physically, but all she remembers is always being pushed off his lap when she was a little girl. Debbie does not remember her family ever doing things together. Usually her mother and the children went out without the father.

Debbie is not sure how her parents got on when she was very young, but thinks they may have been fairly happy. She remembers the last two years before separation as very turbulent with many fights and arguments and her father often coming home drunk in the middle of the night. On some of these occasions, for no apparent reason, he dragged the children as well as his wife out of bed. Debbie remembers feeling frightened and is one of the very few children who wished that their parents would split up.

Debbie believes that what was happening between her parents had a very bad effect on her. She was unable to concentrate and her school work suffered. She was short-tempered and moody with her friends and they could not understand her behaviour. She even had to give up her favourite activity, riding, as she kept falling off the horses. One day Debbie would like to work in a stable or be a jockey... "anything to do with horses".

Debbie knew, while her parents were still married, that her father had a girlfriend, a married woman for whose children Debbie feels sorry as because of the woman's morals she does not consider her a good mother. Debbie used to see this woman and her father together at football matches and one day found a letter her father had written to her. Debbie tried to intervene and told the woman to leave her father alone. When Debbie's parents split up, her mother said it was because of arguments and another woman, which was something Debbie already knew. She thinks that her mother should have "chucked my father out much sooner instead of trying to talk to him and considering seeing a social worker or Marriage Guidance or somebody like that." Whenever Debbie's mother asked her father about his girlfriend he denied that he had one, even though everyone, including Debbie, knew about her. Debbie is very angry with her father for pushing her away as he used to do and for letting them down and upsetting her mother. She used to write on her bedroom wall, "I hate my father." Now when he calls she goes upstairs and refuses to see him. He still calls to see her brother.

Financially, the family are better off since the separation because of the mother's generous disposition. Debbie knows that her mother earns less than her father and he does not pay much maintenance, if any. Debbie's father is a bank manager, her mother manages the local launderette. At first Debbie did not like to ask her mother for anything, but now knows that she can and her mother will not refuse her anything she can afford.

Debbie's mother hardly ever goes out. Debbie would like her to have a better social life and Debbie herself now has many good friends. When she has any worries she can talk to her mother, her friends, and also "a lady down the road". She does not talk much with her brothers and does not like her older brother as much as she used to before he moved out.

One day Debbie may get married. She knows people who are happily married and does not think all marriages are like her parents'. Asked what effect her parents' divorce has had on her Debbie's reply was: "I am much happier... more settled at school. I have got a lot more friends and I am a lot happier."

Young people in the age range twelve to seventeen were obviously at a very different stage of intellectual development to that of the children at infant and primary schools. They had acquired the ability to reason rationally, and to comprehend more fully the meaning of various events, their causes, and consequences. They were often able to piece together for themselves the reasons for their parents' separation and understood the consequences.

Abstract ideas were understood and often given careful consideration. Adolescents understood the difference between divorce and separation. They understood the permanent nature of their parents' parting. They were often preoccupied with such abstract ideas as justice and rights. These ideas were, for instance, applied to questions of custody and access. They recognized that each person involved had certain rights. Parents were often seen as having the right to see a child even if this interfered with the child's timetable. Adolescents thought in terms of compromise and were usually able to see the situation from various points of view, even when these conflicted with their own.

The judgements and opinions of adolescents, we were told, were on many issues in conflict with those of important adults, including parents. Adolescents no longer necessarily identified and took sides with their parents or saw one parent through the eyes of the other. If they wanted more information they were much more resourceful than young children about getting what they needed to form their opinions.

It was this age group who sometimes seemed very rational and "reasonable" as well as expressing the strongest feelings. Sometimes these were of relief, as when a young person remembered a bad pre-divorce situation coming to an end. They were pleased for themselves as well as on behalf of their parents.

We were often aware of anger when talking to adolescents. This was based on their own judgement, not necessarily that of the other parent, or who the "guilty" party was. Even though the law no longer judges one party to be "guilty", adolescents often did apportion guilt. They were angry with parents for rejecting them and with those who had treated the other parent badly. The moral judgements of adolescents were sometimes harsh as, for instance, when the mother or father broke up the marriage to live with or marry someone else. Adolescents seldom saw that there were "two sides to every story". Their feelings often overpowered their ability to think rationally. They also quickly translated their feelings into action, such as by refusing to see a visiting parent or going to one they wanted to visit, without necessarily telling the other.

Adolescents had acquired a wide enough vocabulary to express a variety of emotions and to describe events in detail. Those who remembered well the sequence of events leading up to the final separation gave us vivid descriptions of feelings and events. These were often highly loaded emotionally and reflected the ability to recall and acknowledge very mixed feelings and to recount them accurately.

The range of ways in which adolescents coped with their feelings and situations was wide. They talked to parents, other adults, and friends. This was the first stage at which there was awareness of sources of help outside the family. Adolescents mentioned potential sources such as social workers, Marriage Guidance Counsellors, home helps and various clubs. Their existence was not known to younger children, unless they had actually had contact with them.

It was in adolescence that parents were seen as people in their own right, not just as mothers and fathers. Adolescents were aware of it when parents had worries or when they were happy. They had a great deal of concern for the parents, both for the parents' and their own sake. They liked their parents to have a good social life if it made them happy, but also because it made the young people feel that they themselves were free to go out and enjoy themselves.

Adolescents were sensitive to relationships and to changes in them. We were given detailed accounts of how adolescents got on with parents. They referred to the usual "ups and downs", but saw divorce as making a difference. Living with a single parent either meant that there was only one set of rules and greater consistency or that rules were rigid with no one to take the child's side. Many referred to greater closeness than in two-parent families. To some this was a source of comfort, for others "too close for comfort".

Adolescents analysed for us the impact of divorce on their relationship with their parents. We were given examples of some relationships which improved through seeing parents separately. There were others which became more strained and distant.

The world of adolescents consists not only of the people they live with, but relatives, neighbours, friends, acquaintances, teachers, and many others they meet through belonging to clubs or pursuing hobbies. These people can be a source of direct help and support and were highly valued by adolescents who did not get on too well with those at home or did not like to burden their single parent with worry and were unable to turn to the absent parent. For some, friends provided additional support even when this was available at home.

Having a wide circle of friends and the adolescent's need to conform to what is acceptable to the peer group was sometimes seen as having a negative aspect. Young people being brought up by single parents, who were not able to afford fashionable clothes or school outings and exchange visits abroad, were acutely aware of the differences between themselves and others. Being a member of a closely knit peer group, we were told, had its advantages and disadvantages. Significant and long-lasting friendships were most often mentioned by adolescents.

Many young people in this age group, especially as they approached the school-leaving age, were giving serious consideration to their plans. They thought about jobs and whether or not they wanted to stay on at school. It was at this stage that they realized that they must take their parent's financial position into account in their decisions. Some young people spoke of not wanting to be a financial burden to their parent, or of wanting to get a job and help them. Some expressed worry about the prospect of leaving home and wondered how their parent would cope with living alone if he or she had not remarried and had no stable relationship.

Most young people spoke about their growing need for independence. They told us how they liked to choose their friends and how they spent their time. They wanted to be trusted and have their opinions valued. They wanted their own arrangements taken into account by parents when other family arrangements such as access were being made. At the same time adolescents expressed their need for a secure home base. It was not so much the parent's physical presence that was constantly required, but being sure that parents were available and managing, and the child knowing what to expect and how to relate both to the full-time and the part-time parent.

## Young adults aged eighteen to twenty-four

### David

David, a twenty-one-year-old student, shares a flat with his sister. He has many friends and enjoys cooking for them. He welcomed the interviewer with warmth and enthusiasm and as they both sat comfortably on David's large cushions, David related his story.

It was a late summer afternoon, twelve years before. David had been sitting in the rhubarb patch at the bottom of his garden. He sat there for a long time crying and many thoughts passed through his mind. His father had just left the house after one of his infrequent visits. He had a sad look on his face after saying 'good-bye' to the children. There was something final about the way he said it and yet it was like all the other times. He did not say anything to indicate that he would not be returning.

After Father had gone, David's mother called the children into the kitchen one at a time, the eldest first and the youngest last. While his mother was talking to his older sister David knew what she was going to say. He did not know how and why he knew. His mother told him that she and his father had decided to separate as they did not get on well together any more.

As David sat crying in the rhubarb patch he thought about his father, who rarely came to the house. He travelled a great deal "as a salesman of ideas for surgical instruments", often to America. He had a phoney American accent and often made promises of taking the whole family on holiday to the United States. This was only one of the many promises that were never kept.

David never compared his family with other families he knew; it did not occur to him to ask why his father spent so little time at home. It all seemed so 'ordinary'. David thought about his mother, his brothers and sisters and how well they had always got on. He remembered his father's home-comings. There would be arguments between his parents. His father would send the children out to buy sweets and by the time they came back the parents were kissing and holding hands.

David also remembered poverty and isolation. He had had to share a bed with two of his brothers. His mother's side of the family were well off, but there was no contact with them and no financial help. His mother was well educated and came from a middle-class family. His father was working-class and had had little formal education. In retrospect, David thinks his mother's side of the family disapproved of his father who had attracted his mother by his charm and the fact that they were so different.

As David walked back from the rhubarb patch to the house, he somehow knew that his mother would manage and that he could rely on her. He still had his brothers and sisters. David was nine at this time and he did not see his father again for a long time. He is not sure whether he missed him or what exactly his feelings for his father were. He thought of him mostly as "a goodies man" and remembered all the unfulfilled promises.

As soon as his father had gone his grandparents came to the rescue financially. There was no longer any shortage of money and no debts to worry about, as there had been before. David had his own bed to sleep in. Although David knew that at times his mother was lonely and upset she never tried to lean on the children. They could always go to her for support and comfort. David described his relationship with his mother as extremely significant and positive. It sustained him through many difficulties.

When David was sixteen he and his brothers and sisters were pleased that his mother had decided to marry a well-to-do farmer. After the wedding they moved to their stepfather's farmhouse. Six months after the wedding, delight turned to dismay and terrible disappointment. The stepfather was in some ways like their father, rough and self-assured. Unlike their father, he was also violent and cruel. David witnessed many violent fights and would rush to his mother's defence. Hatred grew between David and his stepfather and there were murderous thoughts in David's mind. He experienced a strong desire to kill his sleeping stepfather, who often threatened David with a shotgun and kept his Alsatian dogs on a chain long enough to frighten the children when they were getting out of the car in the driveway, but just not long enough to allow the dogs to attack them.

One day, on arriving home from school, David, much to his relief, found a removal van outside. The family moved to a new address. When their stepfather eventually found them he appeared penitent and grief-stricken, but David's mother was firm in her resolution never to return to him.

David did not meet his own father again and did not know where he was until he was nineteen. By that time he had met one of his father's several wives' and deduced that either his parents had never been married or his father was a bigamist. He learned about his father's criminal record and that he had been in prison. David now thinks about his father with compassion and has no other feelings for him.

At twenty-one David is a caring, enthusiastic person who enjoys many things. He believes that his parents' separation has had a mainly positive effect on him. It has made him aware that there are many different kinds of families and that children growing up in one-parent families can be provided with the warmth and security which they need. It has helped him to empathize with both children and adults and to be tolerant. He has much compassion and accepts people for what they are. He appreciates the value of good and lasting relationships and has translated this into how he feels about his girlfriend.

★

Young adults shared with us their reflections on how they saw their parents as individuals and how these two separate people got on together. It was only now that much thought seemed to be given to the parents as a couple and the nature of this relationship fully acknowledged, including its sexual component. It was only grown-up children who spoke to us about their knowledge and the fantasies that they had about their parents' sexual relationship. They themselves were at a stage of life when they were giving a great deal of thought to long-term couple relationships, both in relation to others and to themselves. Many felt that they needed to understand what brought their parents together, how they got on and why they had to separate. They felt they could learn from their parents' mistakes and, by knowing what went wrong, avoid the same pitfalls. Many expressed the view that their own marriages would be different.

It was also at this age that many shared with us their scepticism about marriage. Some did so with regret. They wanted to be close to someone, but also were afraid that it would not work.

Many young adults expressed very tolerant views about their parents. They tried to justify behaviour considered difficult or unacceptable. They were far less likely to blame one of the parents for the breakup of the marriage and saw it usually in terms of failure to adapt to each other and meet each other's needs.

## Adults aged twenty-five and over

### Marion

Marion is thirty-seven. She considers herself happily married and has two children. Now that they are both old enough, she intends to return to full-time education.

Marion was born in a small seaside village and has some very happy early memories: playing with friends on the beach and making sand-castles. Yet overall, she described her childhood as "unhappy and frightened". She remembers her mother as "an unhappy, highly-strung woman" who tried to commit suicide. Marion remembers always being afraid of what she might find when she came home from school or visiting friends.

Marion does not now think that her parents' marriage could ever have been happy. "She was a conventional woman married to an unconventional man. He was the original beatnik born before his time ... always spending money on records and playing jazz. He would bring home a bottle of wine and leave my mother short of money for food."

Marion remembers hating her father for making her mother unhappy. She was aware that he was seeing a woman, but "it was all hushed up, in those days people did not talk about divorce". Because they lived in a small village Marion's parents did not want anyone to know what was happening. She is not sure when exactly they separated or if they were ever legally divorced.

From the time when Marion was seven her father only came home at weekends. There were always quarrels and his visits decreased in frequency. She does not remember his visiting after she was twelve. At the time she did not miss him and took her mother's side entirely. She only saw her father once more, at a railway station when she was seeing off her future husband. Her father did not see her.

Neither of Marion's parents ever explained to her that they were separated. Marion remembers her uncle trying to talk to her as he probably realized how unhappy she was but she always successfully avoided the issue. She has tried at various times to talk about her parents or to her sister, but without much success as her sister finds it too upsetting.

Following the separation the family were quite poor. Marion had to go without many things that her friends had, such as new clothes and holidays. "The worst day was when my mother told me the bailiffs were coming to the house ... all the time I was at school and at my friend's house I kept thinking about it." The crisis was averted with the help of the mother's employer.

Marion has always felt responsible for her mother. She left school at sixteen to do a secretarial course although she had wanted to stay on at school and go to university. Later on she turned down a well-paid job as this would have meant leaving home and when she eventually did leave she described it as "The hardest thing I ever did." Since the separation Marion's mother has not been interested in men. Marion would have liked her to remarry. "If she did it would be the happiest day of my life."

Marion thinks that her parents' separation has had a deep and lasting affect on her. She bitterly regrets the loss of contact with her father and having talked with one of his friends thinks that he was an interesting and nice person, but not a suitable husband for her mother.

Marion has grown up with a sense of insecurity and lacks confidence. She is afraid to enjoy herself in case the good things do not last. She thinks that if things had been discussed and explained more fully to her, and if she had not lost contact with her father, who is now dead, she would have grown up into a happier and more confident person.

★

It was from older adults that we learned how long-lasting the effects of separation can be. We were told about feelings of sadness and anger that were stored up for a long time and only emerged in adulthood. Those who lost a parent they loved, or perhaps they did not get a chance to know well and did not grieve for at the time, grieved many years later.

Children who got on well with a parent after divorce were not likely to be on bad terms with them when they grew up. The reverse sometimes happened. Adults who did not get on well with their parents as children spoke of the relationship improving as the years went by. This was also true of step-parents.

Many adults aged twenty-five and over were themselves married and had children. They talked about the effect of divorce on their own marriage. There were those who were desperately eager to create what they did not have as children: a happy marriage and a happy home. Because of this eagerness they did not look around long enough and married in haste. They were not happy with their choice and thought they could have done better. They shared with us their disappointment.

A number were pleased with their choice and their marriage. They invested all they had in it: high hopes and a determination to succeed. For them it had worked. They valued their marriage and their children. They felt fulfilled and that they had found what they had lacked before. They were close to husband or wife and able to communicate well with them.

From the older adults we learned how punitive attitudes to divorce affected their lives as children and adolescents. We were told about feelings of shame, of trying to hide the fact that parents were divorced, and sometimes their total ignorance of divorce at all as parents were afraid to mention it. We were told about teachers and other adults who, having extracted from the child the information that the child had divorced parents, used it in a cruel and punitive way. Divorce was remembered as a subject not to be talked about, a dark secret.

We have in this chapter stressed the difference between age groups in their understanding and reactions to divorce. For each group there were common themes. Yet it is our impression that there were striking similarities between age groups and reactions to similar circumstances which were common to all age groups. This we have emphasized throughout the book.

## Notes and suggested reading

A developmental framework was assumed throughout. For an outline of this the reader is referred to the following selected bibliography:

Bee, H. (1978): *The Developing Child*. London: Harper and Row.

Mussen, P. H & Conger, J. J. (1980): *Readings in Child and Adolescent Psychology*. London: Harper and Row.

Rayner, E. (1978): *Human Development*. London: George Allen and Unwin.

# CHAPTER 4

# I WISHED WE COULD HAVE TALKED MORE

'"There is no sort of use in knocking,' said the Footman, 'and that for two reasons. First, because I'm on the same side of the door as you are, secondly, because they're making such a noise inside, no one could possibly hear you."'
(Lewis Carroll, *Alice's Adventures in Wonderland*.)

How and when children find out that their parents are splitting up, how they react to the news and what they think about the quality of communication about divorce are the main themes under the heading: "I wish we could have talked more."

In recent years good communication has come to be rated highly as an ingredient of happy marriage and satisfactory family relationships. Poor communication is said to be a major cause of tension and breakdown in relationships between husbands and wives and parents and children. Communication in families has received much attention from the media, from those who are involved in various forms of family and marital counselling, and in the literature on family interaction.[1]

Families differ in their patterns of communication and the extent to which things are discussed. In some families most things are talked about. This can happen at special times such as at meals, on arriving home from school or from work, or at bedtime. Many events are shared by all members of the family but individuals and parents as a couple have their secrets. In other families there are no special times. Hardly anyone bothers to say anything or else everyone talks at the same time. Nobody seems interested in listening to anybody but themselves. Poor communication is characterized by inability to share, to listen and by confusion.

Most families are somewhere between the two extremes. Certain things are talked about; others, like sex, are taboo subjects. All families have their share of 'secrets'. It is never easy to talk about painful feelings or to discuss really controversial matters.

Good communication enhances the quality of life. It is a means of conveying needs and showing concern. When different points of view are put forward compromise is possible. When needs cannot be met or conflict resolved good communication can make parting easier and less bitter. Paradoxically, when the need to talk is greatest it is often the most difficult time to do it. When a family is breaking up is often the moment when communication between husbands and wives and between parents and children has failed. This is so in all kinds of families, including those in which previously parents and children were able to talk about almost anything.

Facing children with the announcement that the parents are splitting up is a daunting task. There are many reasons for this which have been described in the growing volume of literature on divorce.[2] Some of the reasons are to do with the nature of the process of separation. Others are connected with uncertainty about how to involve the children. The decision to part is often made after a long period of indecision during which hope alternates with despair and promises with recrimination. During that time parents do not like to worry their children and tend to deny that there is anything wrong. Once the decision has been made it can take anything from a few minutes to several months to put it into practice. Some couples stay together while one or both are looking for somewhere else to live. Others choose a trial separation. When a marriage is breaking up is for adults a time of hurt and angry feelings, shattered hopes, diminished self-worth as well as a time when hope and relief are experienced. Parents are preoccupied with themselves yet at the same time they are anxious to do whatever is best for the children. It is hard to know what to say to a child and what is 'right' timing. Parents may realize that children of different ages need different kinds of explanation. There is uncertainty about how much a child can grasp and how much he or she may already have guessed without being told. Parents wonder how much children want to know and to what extent they should be protected by not being told anything or not being told the truth.

For no two children are the circumstances and the way in which they learn about divorce the same even if they belong to the same family. Age and individual temperament are two of the factors which influence how children react to big changes. We found that the similarities seemed to outweigh the differences. Children of different ages described very similar feelings and reactions at the time of separation. We were told what children wanted to know and what they would have preferred not to hear. There was a clear link between how children reacted to the news and how they remembered and regarded their parents together. Another clear connection emerged between what information children were given and how they responded and dealt with their reactions both during the crisis and after it was over.

We can best describe children's reactions to separation at least partly in their own words. The examples chosen are typical and represent children who were of different ages at the time of separation. They include both those who were dissatisfied in various degrees as well as those who were satisfied with the quality of communication about divorce.

Rosie's story was typical of children who were told very little at the time of separation and following it and whose parents blamed each other for the failure of their marriage. It illustrates both short and long-term consequences of bad communication. Rosie's words, "I wish we could have talked more," were echoed in different ways by the majority of those to whom we spoke.

Rosie, now in her thirties, considers herself happily married to a builder. She has young children. She does not go out to work, preferring to be a full-time housewife. She replied to our advertisement in the local paper. As Rosie and the interviewer began to talk in Rosie's comfortable sitting-room Rosie pointed to a Welsh dresser and said it had belonged to her 'Gran' and then to her 'Dad'. During the interview Rosie looked back over many years. She told us: "Everything in all those years is still with me."

Rosie has no memories of her parents being happy together. "They should have done it much sooner," said Rosie, from a distance of twenty years, though she did not think so at the time. "They stayed together and waited until we were much older. My dad was a travelling salesman. He always had to have another woman as well as my mum. She was in a wheelchair with arthritis and was aggravated by this as well as my dad. They argued a lot. It was usually my mum who did the picking. I usually took Dad's side. My sister was older and knew more about Dad's woman. She knew more about what was going on.

"When I was fifteen everything changed. I remember my Mum hitting my dad with a bottle of H.P. sauce. She hit him on the head. Every time I see a bottle of H.P. sauce I feel upset." As Rosie's father stormed out of the house Rosie hid in his car hoping to go with him for a drive. When some time later she returned to the house, cold and in tears, she was told by her mother that her father would not be coming back. Rosie felt upset, lost, and bewildered. She did not like to ask questions but listened to her mother's accusations against her father. This made her even more unhappy and for a time she took her mother's side. She also missed her father, did not know where he was, and did not have the courage to inquire for fear of upsetting her mother. She also felt unwanted by her father and thought she was a burden to her mother. She resented the fact that her older sister and her mother were very close and seemed to discuss things that were not shared with Rosie. As far as Rosie was concerned "nothing was ever discussed … they did not sit down with me and talk about it all properly."

Eventually, Rosie screwed up enough courage to visit her grandmother in the hope of contacting her father and found him living there. He told her that he was about to get married. This came as a surprise to Rosie and a disappointment as Rosie had hoped to move in with her father. Soon after this her sister also got married and took over the family home while Rosie's mother moved out to live with a man to whom Rosie had taken an instant dislike. These plans had not been discussed with Rosie and she was only told at the last minute.

At sixteen, feeling unwanted by all, Rosie moved in with a young drug addict who treated her badly and was always demanding her wages. Eventually Rosie moved in with her grandmother, and got on well again with her father while she became more and more resentful about the complaints her mother was always making about him. At no point was Rosie quite sure to whom she could be close and turn for help and advice.

Since Rosie got married at eighteen she has had a great deal of security and happiness. Yet the feeling of insecurity is still with her. For this she blames both parents and their failure to explain what was happening at the time of separation and afterwards. Rosie is afraid of the dark. She does not like being alone. When her family are at home she keeps the doors in the flat open so that she can feel close to her husband and children. She finds their presence reassuring.

Rosie finished the interview by saying: "They should have told us more … in my family, my husband and my children, we talk about everything."

Another child who remembered many rows yet was surprised when his mother left the house was Marc, a twenty-two-year-old student, who was eight when it happened. Marc was able to describe in detail all the conflicting feelings which he remembered having at the time.

"My mother had a boyfriend, but I did not think anything of it at the time. I remember the day she left. I had lots of feelings of hatred towards the guy she was going to live with. There was also a feeling of relief. There had been arguments, lots of arguments, it was absolute hell. After she left my father went to pieces, he started to drink heavily. She never said anything about it before she went. The arguments were having an effect on me. There were pictures in my mind, torn pictures, fear of what would happen to me. Whenever I was naughty my parents threatened me with boarding-school. I was afraid I would be sent away. My parents never explained. I picked up what was going on. It was my grandmother making moral recriminations against my mother. The insecurity about the future was overwhelming."

Marc's unhappiness continued for a long time throughout his father's second marriage until, as a young adult, Marc resumed contact with his mother whom he loves very much and who now lives on her own.

Accusations and recriminations were not only directed at parents, but some children were made to feel that they had also played a part in the break-up of the marriage. The devastating effect of such accusations is illustrated by Barbara. Barbara's parents parted when she was thirteen. At eighteen she has still not fully recovered from the effects of what she considers was the worst possible way to learn about separation. Until recently Barbara could remember very little about the events surrounding separation and she tried to deny that she had any feelings about it. She regained her memory and the ability to feel with a great deal of help from the school counsellor whom she had been seeing regularly.

Barbara is an only child. She remembered her mother as always having been possesive and resentful of any close contact between Barbara and her father. Barbara was one of the very few children who were aware that a parent was having an affair. Her mother's lovers often stayed overnight when Barbara's father was away from home. Barbara did not think it would be right to tell her father about her mother's affairs. Burdened with her secret and guilt she was never able to face her parents together and would burst into tears and run out of the room. Her parents could not understand her behaviour and became angry. In turn Barbara came to feel that all the rows they were having were about her.

It was Barbara's father who eventually asked for a divorce when he met a woman he fell in love with. "He got all the blame," which Barbara felt was unfair since she considered her mother equally guilty of breaking up the marriage. Barbara's feelings of guilt were reinforced by her mother's accusations that her behaviour had helped to break up the marriage and that Barbara should have tried harder to keep her father at home. Divorce was not what Barbara's mother had wanted or anticipated.

Throughout her adolescence Barbara has been an unhappy, lonely girl. She has not got on well with her mother since the separation and her relationship with her father became more distant than before. When he visits they mostly sit in his car in silence. It is only now that Barbara can enjoy certain things, has some good friends, and some faint hope that one day she may be able to talk to her father, "but that day still seems very far off".

Danny and Helen were two of the children too young at the time of separation to be told or to understand what was happening. Both realized when they were between three and four years old that they had another parent somewhere in the world whom they did not know. Like most children in this position they felt sad and curious about the absent parent, manifesting their feelings in different ways.

Danny was fourteen years old when we met him. His sadness was evident. He has not questioned his father about his mother, who left him when he was a baby. When Danny was about three his father showed him a photograph of his mother and a letter. All that Danny knows about his mother is who she looked like some years ago and her handwriting. He has not asked his father for more information as he does not like to cause him pain by resurrecting the past. The reason that Danny was given for the divorce was that his parents did not agree.

Helen, in her late twenties, remembers a man who took her out long before she was old enough to be at school. She was later told that this was her father. Her mother did not speak well of him. Unlike Danny, who gets on well with his father, Helen did not get on well with her mother. In her adolescence she made determined, though unsuccessful, efforts to be reunited with her father. Her failure caused great pain and anger. It is only very recently that she was told by a friend 'to bury the past' and was able to do so.

Judy belongs to a group of children who were told very little about separation and neither resented this lack of communication nor were made unhappy by it. Judy, aged seventeen, told us that her parents were in a residential job together. When the Home in which they worked closed down the parents got jobs in different localities and Judy went with her mother. Her father's visits became less and less frequent. One Christmas Judy became aware that her parents were sleeping in separate beds. She commented on this and was told that they had been divorced for some time. Judy was not surprised or upset as she had become used to seeing little of her father and they had gradually drifted apart. Judy had always been close to her mother and has got on well with her.

Tina and Janet two of the few children who were pleased with the way they had been told about divorce. We were told by fourteen-year-old Tina: "I knew something was wrong. I heard arguments when I was in bed, and I cried... I did not know too much because I was too young to know what it was about. My mother was depressed. She had to wear glasses, dark glasses because she was always crying." Tina described her life at the time as pretty miserable.

Tina's parents finally decided to separate when Tina (then nine) was away on holiday with her sister staying at their grandmother's house. "When we came back from holiday Mum took us into the front room and told us. I knew something drastic was going to happen so I was crying while we were away. I knew that they were not right together but at that age you cannot really understand properly what is wrong because you cannot really understand that your parents cannot live together. Parents are *there* and this is it as far as you are concerned."

Tina's mother told Tina and her sister that she and their father were not happy and could no longer live together. The sisters would live with their mother and see their father regularly at weekends and during holidays. He would come to visit and take them out, and they could go for holidays. "It was right, but I did not want to accept it. It had to be done but I did not like it."

Looking back Tina feels that her parents made the right decision. "Now my Mum is completely different to what she was then. She cares what she looks like. She does not mind getting up early and facing the day. Father is also quite different, not as quiet as before and generally nicer."

Janet, aged fifteen, whose parents separated when she was eleven, was another one of the few children who spoke positively about communication. She represents the few exceptional families in which the parents were actually able to face the children together and tell them about the separation.

Janet remembers many quarrels while her parents were together. "My Dad used to smash things but the violence was towards things, not the person. I thought it was natural that people argued. I used to feel angry more than upset. I was happy most of the time." When Janet first noticed that her parents had separate beds, when previously they share a double one, she asked why and was told that her father sweated at night and this kept her mother awake. "It was strange. You sort of feel there is something strange. When I was older I asked again and they told me the truth: they did not get on."

Before Janet's parents finally separated she and her brother were involved in some of the discussions. Several possibilities were considered, such as dividing the house into two flats. "We all sat round and talked about it." On the day when her father moved out Janet cried a great deal. "It was a great shock. I really cried. I felt upset but not so upset as my crying would make it seem. I wanted my Dad to go but I did not want him to know I did. The crying just came easily. I felt I was losing my security being left with my Mum who had nothing, no job. She suffers from asthma. When he left I had all these feelings: who would look after me if she was not well? I missed him. At night it was worst because you have time to think ... it was only my Mum. I used to wake up a lot and feel empty inside. I used to feel upset because my Mum was upset."

It was some months before Janet recovered from the shock of the separation. She sees her father and gets on really well with both her parents. This she feels is to a large extent due to the way they involved her in discussions and listened to what she had to say.

Children seemed to learn about divorce at similar stages. Those who were too young at the time of separation to understand what was happening remembered that between the ages of three and four they began to realize that other children had two parents living with them. Many of these children had lost contact with the parent they did not live with. A few had vague memories of a person they eventually learned was their mother or father.

Of the children who were old enough to understand what was happening at the time of separation very few remember being given any warning that their parents were about to split up. It was often on the point of departure, while the mother or father was packing their belongings, that the child was told that he or she was leaving. Some parents left without saying anything and the child only learned later that they would not be coming back.

One-third of the children did not remember ever being told that their parents were separating or had already been divorced. A wall of silence surrounded the person who was no longer there and the circumstances that had led up to separation. Over a period of time these children realized that they had lost a parent and were not likely to see them again. This was often so when a parent was normally away from home a great deal as, for instance, fathers in the Armed Forces or who travelled on business. There were, however, parents who had normally lived with the child all the time whose sudden absence was never explained.

A number of young children remember being told something they could not understand and then very gradually realizing what had happened. We were told by one of these children, Jane (aged eight), that she remembered he mother telling her something about her father when she was four. All Jane could remember was that while her mother was telling her Jane's sister kept interrupting. Jane did not grasp what was being said. She did not ask questions or indicate she could not understand.

It was usually mothers who talked to the children. Since most children stayed with their mothers perhaps the pressure on them to say something was greater than on fathers. All but a few fathers avoided the subject of separation even when questioned later on by their grown-up children. Only a very small number of parents were remembered as being able to face the child together with the news of separation. When both parents did talk to the child they did so separately and on different occasions.

In whatever way children learned about divorce those who were old enough to understand were at first taken by surprise and most found it hard to believe that their parents could not stay together. Divorce was something they had not expected. This applied to children of all ages in all kinds of families. It was true of children who had friends with divorced parents as well as of those who were not even sure what 'divorce' meant. Divorce was something that happened in other children's families. With very few exceptions children neither wished that their parents would split up nor considered it a real possibility.

Such lack of anticipation can only be understood in the context of how children remembered and thought about their parents while they were together. From what we were told it became obvious that children thought about their parents simply as their 'mums' and 'dads' rather than as two married adults who had a relationship with each other. Mothers and fathers were seen as permanent figures who were expected to be there for as long as the child could see ahead. Only grown-up children analysed the nature and quality of the parental relationship and compared it with others.

The word 'ordinary' was one of the most frequently used to describe how children thought of their parents' marriage. This description encompassed many different kinds of relationship. Some parents were remembered as being apparently very happy together. There was a great deal of loving contact between them and they were remembered as kissing and hugging each other. They laughed and joked, went out together and did things together at home. They seemed to share many interests and liked similar things or complemented each other's differences.

There were also parents who existed in an atmosphere of recrimination or even silence. If they ever went out or sat down together to a meal this was a memorable occasion. Children could sense a tense atmosphere even if they were not aware of the reason for it. Many thought that they probably knew more than their parents realized. Children usually noticed signs of distress, as when a parent had been crying or found it hard to get up and face the day. The aftermath of violence, such as bruises and black eyes, was often explained away by parents as due to accidents. They were not always believed.

The most vivid and unhappy memories were of parental fights and arguments. While parents quarrelled late at night in bed children lay awake and listened from a safe distance, feeling frightened and helpless. When parents denied that there was anything wrong the children's insecurity increased. Some children wondered if the arguments were about them and they were in some way to blame. Some thought they were a burden to their parents.

Some children witnessed actual physical violence. This was sometimes directed at objects, but usually the mother was at the receiving end. On occasions children rushed to the defence of one parent or, while trying to stop the fight, got hurt themselves. Some children were quite severely punished when their parents felt angry with each other and needed to vent frustration.

We were given many examples of fights and arguments remembered in minute detail even when other memories had faded. Diane, aged twenty-two, whose parents separated when she was ten, was one example. She described in detail the colour and shape of a chair on which she used to stand while pleading with her parents to stop arguing. She also remembers well her feelings of fear and helplessness.

However tense and unhappy was the atmosphere at home and however aware children were that their parents did not agree, children did not think of divorce as a remedy. They wished that their parents would stop quarrelling and for a more peaceful and predictable way of life. It was only when looking back that children realized that they might have been asking for the impossible.

The feelings that children remembered having at the time of separation seemed to be most intense when they first learned about it. Although there was some variation with age and circumstances, many children mentioned very similar feelings and reactions. Many were confused and had highly conflicting feelings, such as wanting their parents to stay together and yet feeling pleased and relieved because a bad situation had been resolved.

The world the child has known is about to change when parents decide to part. Whether happy or threatening, that world was at least familiar. When it seems to be collapsing the future is unknown. This is how the children themselves described in retrospect their reaction when they first knew about the separation. Many remembered feeling very unhappy. They could not enjoy the things they normally did or look forward to treats. They were apathetic, could not get to sleep, woke up in the night and lost their appetite. Some children expressed their misery by crying both at home and at school. Others remember trying to hide their feelings and being very quiet and withdrawn. Misery was also manifested as bad temper.

A high number of children felt very insecure. They were worried about which parent they would live with, particularly if they thought they might have to live with the one they liked less. Children were worried how a single parent would manage to look after them, specially if the parent had no job or was not well. Children who loved and were attached to the parent who was going away worried in case they would not see him or her often or not at all. Children wondered if both parents would go on loving them as they had done before. They were also not quite sure how to regard a part-time parent – could they still confide in them and ask them for things?

Anger was a reaction most common in adolescence. Children in their teens felt angry with parents who deserted them or who in their judgement had caused the breakup of the marriage. This anger was expressed sometimes as a rejection of the 'guilty' parent and a refusal to see them if they came to visit.

A number of children, specially those whose parents divorced before more permissive attitudes to divorce began to prevail, tried to hide the fact that the parents were separating. They felt that having a 'broken home' was shameful and made the child different. Children who lived in closely knit communities or whose family had religious beliefs condemning divorce were particularly prone to feeling stigmatized. Young children particularly felt that they had to take sides. Whereas an older child might go and see a mother or a father without permission or the approval of the other parent, younger children felt that they needed to take the side of the parent on whom they were more dependent. They found themselves reflecting this parent's attitude.

A significant number of children felt great relief. A bad situation had come to an end. There would be no more quarrelling and violence. Children hoped that one or both their parents might be happier apart than together. They would no longer have to cope with the tension or uncertainty, or try to protect a parent. They hoped the atmosphere at home would be more peaceful and that they could concentrate on their homework without having to worry about what was happening at home while they were at school or with friends.

Not all children greeted the news of separation with feelings of either dismay or relief. There were those who remembered feeling quite indifferent. For some children separation did not bring any great changes. One of the parents might have been away from home a great deal and the child had got used to only having one parent there every day. Not all children were equally close to both parents; some were used to the company of one parent while the other was regarded almost as a stranger. The parent with whom a child had very limited contact was not missed in the same way as a parent to whom a child was strongly attached.

Many children experienced conflicting emotions on receiving the news of separation and mentioned a variety of reactions which are summarized in the table below – as far as it is possible to define complex feelings surrounding an important event.

| | |
|---|---|
| Feeling unhappy | 57 |
| Crying | 28 |
| Feeling bewildered | 23 |
| Feeling relieved | 22 |
| Feeling 'different to others' | 22 |
| Wanting to take sides and blame one parent | 15 |
| Feeling insecure | 15 |
| Feeling indifferent | 15 |
| Feeling shattered | 13 |
| Feeling guilty | 11 |
| Feeling depressed | 6 |

★

The children and adults to whom we spoke experienced little difficulty in telling us how they felt about separation. Very few remembered talking to their parents and believed that the parents did not know how they felt. Children did not like to worry their parents. They felt protective towards them. Somehow, the children felt, it was not right to ask questions. Children did not remember being given many opportunities to express how they felt or being encouraged to talk about what was happening. Whereas communication is normally a two-way process it appeared that children in most families were passive recipients of what parents chose to tell them and that they were observers rather than participants in the process although this was of such vital concern to them.

The questions and anxieties which children had were mostly to do with their current feelings and the future. Parents mostly seemed to be talking about the past and the reason for the separation. Children did have some curiosity about the fact that their parents could not go on being together, but were usually satisfied with quite a simple explanation which might not be satisfactory to an adult, as was demonstrated by the adult children to whom we spoke. For some there came a stage when they wanted to know much more about their parents' marriage and divorce than they had been told when they were children.

How children came to view the reasons for the separation also included what others outside the family said and sometimes overheard conversations as well. When this information was processed several pieces of the jigsaw puzzle were fitted together. The younger the child the greater the tendency to accept whatever the parents said.

The explanations which children gave for their parents separation were expressed differently by different age-groups, but they conveyed similar ideas which can be grouped under headings. Arguments and the existence of a boyfriend or a girlfriend were top of the list. Both were mentioned by just over half the volunteers. Other reasons were mentioned less frequently

| | |
|---|---|
| They had arguments | 55 |
| Mother/father had a boyfriend/girlfriend | 51 |
| They were not compatible | 41 |
| There was violence | 17 |
| They had grown apart | 13 |
| Mother/father was ill | 13 |
| No reason known | 13 |

★

In a number of cases divorce was thought to have been caused by several factors, none of which on its own would have been sufficient to break up a marriage. Whenever only one reason could be thought of it was always 'arguments'. When parents said they were breaking up because of arguments, children were not surprised. Arguments seemed to be an acceptable reason, though some children were aware that most couples argue, yet nevertheless stay together. Other reasons that were given to children and remembered by them as causing arguments were questions of money, going out alone, and drinking. When parents mentioned other partners as the cause of quarrels many children had not known about this until they were actually told. In a few cases children were told that they themselves were the cause of disagreements. Of course this was very upsetting.

A large number of children were told directly that one or both parents were having or had had an affair. This was usually said bitterly and was greeted by the child with some surprise since not many of even the older children were aware of, or wanted to acknowledge, the sexual nature of what they considered were friendships. Parents who were jilted for another man or woman often spoke of their spouse in highly derogatory terms and such words as 'bitch' and 'bastard' were often used within a child's hearing. Children were usually very upset by this, but not many were able to defend an absent parent.

Incompatibility was a word not always used, but the idea was conveyed in a variety of ways. Some of the phrases used were: "they were not right together", "they had nothing in common", "they did not go well together", "they were not well suited", "my mum went out on Mondays, Wednesdays and Fridays, my dad went out on Tuesdays, Thursdays and Saturdays. On Sundays they either took it in turns or stayed at home. They never enjoyed doing things together". Children had often observed these things for themselves before adults put them into words. "Not being right together" did not make anyone into a guilty party and did not create for the child a situation of divided loyalty. It was a highly acceptable explanation and enabled the child to continue a relationship with both parents without guilt or awkwardness.

Violence as an explanation hardly needed to be mentioned. Children were aware of it even at an early age. They were usually very sympathetic to a parent who suffered as a result of violence and relieved when a violent parent left.

Physical and mental illness were given as reasons in a small number of cases. Those who were permanently disabled or suffered pain told the children that their spouse was not able to tolerate this and the restrictions which ill-health and lack of mobility can impose. Children usually felt sympathetic towards the disabled parent and angry with the parent who deserted them.

Some parents were said to be abnormally depressed or suspicious or their behaviour was particularly difficult. They were described as mentally ill and in some cases were undergoing psychiatric treatment. Heavy drinkers were often remembered as such. Drinking was the cause of violent, unpredictable, and embarrassing behaviour which beyond a certain point could not be tolerated. Like children in violent marriages, children in alcoholic marriages seemed to have few regrets about the marriage breaking up although some felt concern for the parent they considered to be ill or in need of help.

Some parents had originally got on well. Children were pleased to know this. It was over a period of time that parents changed and developed different interests and ambitions. Some partners who were passive and prepared to be dominated became more independent and resented being the weaker partner although this had suited them originally. Others developed different aspirations from those they had when they married. One partner no longer shared the other's ambitions nor fitted in with a new circle of friends. Children were told, and older ones saw for themselves, how their parents grew apart.

Some children did not seem to know why their parents separated. They did not remember this ever being explained and they themselves had never asked. They displayed a lack of curiosity. However, these were in a minority. More children were dissatisfied with what they were told or not told by their fathers than by their mothers. Quality of explanation, not quantity, was important. Some parents said a great deal, but this was seen mainly as giving him or her the chance to vent anger and frustration rather than to give the child proper information.

A small number of children were very appreciative of the sensitive and considerate way in which their parents had talked to them. Children whose parents spoke to them together, or had at least both spoken to the child separately, were pleased about this. This did not happen very often and such parents seemed to be the exception.

Older children displayed some understanding of their parents' motives and reasons for not handling the situation well. Children who had been lied to, for instance, thought this was done to protect them. Similar reasons were given in parents' favour by children who were assured that all was well when it was not. From the child's point of view the end did not justify the means and they would have preferred truth and honesty.

It would be wrong to suggest that all children were resentful and unhappy when they were not involved in the discussions about separation and left to find out for themselves. Some at least appeared to be quite content with this. They might have been very young when parents separated and grown up with another adult whom they accepted as a parent, or the process of losing touch with a parent was gradual and the main attachment continued to be to the parent with whom the child was living. If these children were curious and unhappy because of knowing little or nothing they did not show this in obvious ways and may not have been aware of all the feelings they had at the time. The majority of children are unhappy at the time, but many were able to deal with unhappiness and adjust well to a new situation. Others carry their unhappiness through the whole period of growing up into adulthood.

The quality of communication at the time of separation was of vital importance to how children coped at the time and for many years to follow. It is also to a large extent determined how parents and children got on after separation. Poor communication had an adverse effect on relationships which were described as having been good before separation. The relationship between children and parents who had not got on well, improved as a result of proper communication.

Communication about separation is to do with reasons, feelings and consequences. We learned that while children were mostly concerned with current feelings and the future, what was said was mostly about the past. The children of divorced parents helped us to understand what children want to know and what they would prefer to do without.

Children do not usually want to know in great detail why their parents are splitting up. Sometimes the reasons are obvious to them anyway. Questioning, analysis and reflection may come when the child has grown up, but even grown-up children respect the privacy of the parental relationship. "What happens between two people is sacred and should not be questioned by anyone." (Eve, aged twenty-two, whose parents separated when she was three). "We argued" or "we did not get on well" seem to be quite satisfactory explanations for a child. Hearing that their parents had once got on well, often brought a smile to a sad child's face.

Children do not want to be put in the position of feeling that they have to take sides with one parent against the other. This expectation can be created in many different ways including denigrating one parent or refusing to talk about them. Children do not want to hear their parents blamed, described as bad or difficult, or to listen to details of their extra-marital affairs or their unsatisfactory sexual relationship. Eventually children come to resent having to take sides or to listen to mutual parental accusations even if they were too young to protest at the time.

There are a number of things that children like to hear and have explained. As most children love both parents they want to be assured that they will continue to have two parents. They need to know that their relationship with each parent is separate from the relationship between the parents themselves and that they need not feel what the parents feel or repeat the parents' words. They need to be reassured that they are not to blame for the marriage breaking up and that a parent is not going away because he or she no longer loves the child or never did.

Children like to be involved in arrangements for custody and access, though there are exceptions to this. They want to know that the parents agree about the arrangements whatever their current relationship. Children need some guidelines about relating to a part-time parent; this is discussed more fully in the chapter on access.

There are parents who are violent and cruel to their children, who destroy a child's confidence and inspire fear. Children need reassurance that they will not be forced to live with a violent parent and that whatever access there is will take account of the child's fear and will be carefully supervised. Children who did not have the opportunity to know a parent well because they were too young at the time the parent disappeared or whose memory is blurred, like some help in getting to know the absent person. Children tend either to idealize or totally reject a mother or a father who is a stranger and need help in building a more realistic image. Letters and photographs as well as talking to someone who knew the person are some of the ways of making the absent parent real to the child. Telling a child about the things the absent parent and the child used to do together establishes a link. The very fact that the parent looking after the child is willing to talk about the other parent is important.

It is to parents that children look for explanations of things they do not understand, for patience and encouragement to ask questions which they find difficult to express. These questions may never be asked without strong encouragement. Children need to be told in so many words that it is all right to ask and that the parent will not be angry. Children often have strange fears about things most unlikely to happen and not intended by the parent, such as immediate remarriage.

There does not seem to be any way of completely avoiding the pain and distress caused by loss and separation. Upset children, each in his or her own way, ask for understanding and attention at the worst possible time from the grown-ups' point of view, when their resources are low. Separation is a time when most parents themselves are unhappy and need help. It is also a time when help given to children can prevent a great deal of damage.

Most of the one hundred children who described their experiences at the time of separation found themselves on the same side of the door as those who might have helped them and yet did not listen to them. From those who were not "on the same side" we discovered the value of good communication. The table below relates the quality of communication as described by the children.

|            | Mother | Father | Both parents together |
|------------|--------|--------|-----------------------|
| None       | 49     | 78     | 91                    |
| Poor       | 19     | 6      | 1                     |
| Acceptable | 14     | 6      | 5                     |
| Good       | 10     | 7      | 1                     |
| Very good  | 8      | 3      | 2                     |
| Total      | 100    | 100    | 100                   |

## Notes and suggested reading

For discussion of communication in families the reader is referred to:

Satir, V. (1972): *Peoplemaking, Science and Behaviour Books*, Palo Alto.

Walrond-Skinner, S. (1976): *Family Therapy*. London: Routledge and Kegan Paul.

Parents' difficulties in communicating with children about divorce are described in the literature on divorce including:

Hart, N., (1976): *When Marriage Ends*. London: Tavistock Publications.

Mitchell, A. K. (1981): *Someone To Turn to*. Aberdeen: Aberdeen University Press.

Wallerstein, J. and Kelly, J. B., (1980): *Surviving the Breakup*. Grant MacIntyre.

# CHAPTER 5

# WHAT HELPS? "THERE NEED TO BE OTHERS"

'Divorce has a great effect upon children. Support from parents or substitutes can counterbalance the loss – not make up for it, but provide an alternative so that children will grow up differently, but satisfactorily. I'm not satisfied with the current attitudes towards children of divorce. They are either regarded as some sort of mistake or they are something to be cosseted. Children need substitutes – people don't realize this. Children don't need more attention from people, one parent doesn't have to be twice as affectionate; there need to be others as well.' This was said by Jonathan, now aged twenty-one, whose parents separated when he was eleven. We asked everyone we interviewed about help in relation to their parents' divorce. Did they need any, did they receive any, from where, or from whom? What sort of help was it? Was it in fact useful?

Children expected help to come from their parents, but in the matter of divorce, very few received it. This chapter therefore looks at the help they received outside the family. Young children had great difficulty in envisaging a situation where they could talk freely to an outsider about their feelings about their parents' separation. They looked to their parents and close family members for this sort of help, but there the subject was often taboo. In fact asking questions even of those they were close to was difficult for many young children to contemplate. They expected that the situation would be explained to them without their having to ask first. Fortunately for some they found help being offered from elsewhere – or they found it for themselves – but others had to do without.

We met only a few children who had had contact with professional helpers at the time of their parents' separation or during the process of the divorce. Most of it was helpful. Valerie was twelve when we met her and she recalled for us her meeting with Miss Jones, two or three years previously.

Miss Jones was a Divorce Court Welfare Officer who was having to prepare a report for the Divorce Court to help the court decide which parent should have custody of Valerie: "I was shocked at the time. I don't think I had ever heard of divorce. I didn't know the meaning of it. I was very angry with both my parents. I didn't want to talk to either of them. I got very uptight about it all – until Miss Jones came. She was ever so nice and understanding, I got it all off my chest talking to her."

Jamie, ten and Dick, eight, spoke in similar terms of the Divorce Court Welfare officer they met, when their parents, like Valerie's, disagreed over custody arrangements. He explained what was happening and they said he was 'very nice' and 'very helpful'.

For the vast majority of those we met the question of help and whether it was available – and actually helpful – seemed a matter of chance and to some extent depended upon how the family saw themselves in relation to the world outside, or perhaps on how they thought the world outside might view them, a family that was separating. Rachel was nine when her parents separated and she was instructed to keep it a secret. "I didn't talk to anyone about my parents separating. I needed to have lots of friends and one special friend – I still do [Rachel is now eighteen]. I didn't talk about home, friends were a total escape from that." Rachel was very angry and shocked about what was happening to her family; she had no idea that her parents were planning to separate. She recalls family members showing their distress and she remembers people crying, but no one outside the family was to know. Rachel then remembers how embarrassed she felt and how, as she put it, she lost confidence in herself.

Molly also tried to keep her parents' separation a secret. She remembers feeling deeply ashamed of the fact that her parents were divorced. These feelings were associated with her Roman Catholic upbringing. Molly was attending a convent school at the time, and she remembers how she tried to hide the facts from everyone, but the nuns teaching her suspected something was wrong and gradually dragged it out of her. Molly was terribly upset by this.

Schools featured very frequently in our discussions about help. Teachers and schools are well placed to be helpful and some did help, although a few of those we met like Molly had painful experiences. "I had just changed schools at eleven when my parents separated," Jonathan said. "I was angry with most people – in fact I was furious. On reflection I do think my school had an understanding attitude and gave me a lot of leeway; they let me be absent, they let me go home if I asked. It did mean that if I really felt terrible and really couldn't face a situation that I could go home. Maybe it wasn't a good thing but it seemed to be a good thing. I wasn't aware of how helpful this was until I didn't need it any more – until I'd grown out of it, until I was just having the same sort of usual problems as all the other kids. It was a large school, they had a pastoral network of teachers, I got understanding, they bent the rules."

Nicola had mixed feelings about how helpful her school was. "The day after my mother left I went into school. I started crying and went to the medical room. I remember telling everything to the teachers – they were very understanding, but then sometimes I used to get to school late and they didn't always believe my reasons." Nicola was then having to keep house for herself and her father.

Barbara eventually made use of the help available from the school counsellor. She had lived an isolated, burdensome life. She remembers her childhood as being miserable and guilt-ridden; when her parents' marriage ended she was fourteen. Barbara felt nothing and was completely rational about everything. Then a year ago when she was seventeen she went to see the counsellor about another matter and found herself talking about her parents' separation and unburdening her feelings about it. "It was upsetting at times but it was helpful. Help based at school makes sense."

Pauline remembers a teacher at her school who was particularly helpful. Pauline's parents' divorce was a particularly acrimonious and split the family members into factions. Pauline had become lonely and isolated. "There was a teacher at school, I shall never forget him. He gave me attention. He was a good listener. I probably didn't want someone to give me advice, just someone to listen."

Not all the children were so fortunate in their schools or their teachers. "There were teachers at school who knew what had happened," said Susan, "but they weren't really interested."

Cynthia, now twenty-one, recalled that she had been happy with the arrangements made for her to live with her maternal grandparents when her parents divorced, and how upset and embarrassed she was when "the teacher suddenly started to ask me in front of the whole class why my name was different from my parents', thinking my grandparents were my real parents."

Dorothy went to boarding-school: "There was no one to help at the time, but there were quite a few children in my school in the same position, so I wasn't a one and only and that was nice – you don't want to be the odd one out do you? It's easier to accept it because others are in the same position."

Friends were of great importance to many of those we met. Just having them there as in the case of Rachel and Dorothy, or friends to talk to was helpful. Many whose parents had divorced during their adolescent years turned to friends of their own age as the chief source of help outside the family. Often these friends were also children of divorced parents and could see things from the same point of view. Janet told us: "I was moody and sullen, no one could speak to me, I'd just growl at them. I was really OK with my best friend. I could only talk to her. I'd tell her everything. There was nothing anyone could do but it helped to talk to her." Even younger children got help from friends, though they were less able to detail the ways in which this happened. Brothers and sisters rarely talked to each other about what was happening to them, rarely confided in each other about how they felt, but knowing that it wasn't only happening to oneself but to them also was described as helpful.

Valerie remembers someone – she doesn't know who – giving her a book to read. It was about a child whose parents were divorcing. "It was a story about a little boy, his parents had argued a lot and they divorced. It was a nice book, I enjoyed reading it, I read it so many times and it helped me at that time when I was nine or ten."

Pauline is in her early twenties now and in addition to her very helpful teacher who was good at listening she found she had poetry inside her. "I was very sad, I was lonely and depressed sitting in a corner just crying and crying. I took a lot of tablets and slept a long time, then I just suddenly started writing poetry. They are terribly depressing morbid poems, but I often think this is how I got the sadness out of me. I don't write poems now. It wasn't that I was so upset about my parents separating, it was a relief at the time, but once it had happened I started thinking things. I used to wander around feeling sorry for my father who was left on his own. Sometimes I came home from just walking around in tears, and sometimes I needed to be on my own to think."

These feelings of aloneness, not knowing if help is needed, and not knowing where to turn if it is, were captured by Paula. Nearing forty now, Paula grew up in her mother's second marriage. Little was explained to her and in fact for some years she was told lies and led to believe that her family circumstances were different from what they actually were. "At the time I felt no one could help. I didn't know I needed help. My mother changed my name to that of her second husband. All through school I was known by his name – I desperately wanted to be known by my real father's surname."

Toby's opinion as he looked back to his childhood was that he probably wouldn't have made use of help even if it had been available. He described himself, now in his early twenties, as an independent person and one suspected that he had lost his trust in adults a long time before. His parents separated when he was two years old and he did not live with either of them: he was placed in the care of the local authority. He remembers social workers asking them questions, but also remembers being too busy wondering why they were asking them to think about the answers – he would usually respond with a 'don't know'. Toby saw a psychiatrist once but he only told Toby how he, Toby, felt and Toby knew this already.

Helen was also distrustful of adults and helpers. She spent some time in local authority care. Helen described her feelings of being ignored as of rarely being seen as a person in her own right. "I was suspicious," she told us, "but it might have been helpful to talk to someone who had some understanding." Some of those we met had reached out for help some years after the distressing experience of their parents' divorce. Usually they were people who had had little or no help with their feelings at the time, but who continued to suffer. Ann told us, "I felt depressed quite often about the situation. I've done a lot of thinking about it and have had to face up to the problems. I never talked to anyone of my own age about the intensely personal things, but later I talked to a minister of the church. He was very understanding, he could say in a few words things which I had been struggling to get sorted out for years – he never made me feel that I was being trivial."

Bewilderment, confusion and anger were among the feelings many experienced on learning that their parents were separating, or if the initial reaction was one of relief the other feelings soon followed. It was these that people needed help with, or with the feelings of depression that followed when the anger had to be hidden away. It is sometimes postulated that it is healthier for feelings to be outwardly expressed. It is seen as rational and to be expected that children will cry if they are hurt, will shout if they get angry, will need comfort if they are in pain. Indeed adults too will have the same needs. "Give sorrow words:" wrote Shakespeare, "the grief that does not speak whispers the o'er fraught heart and bids it break". But so often it seemed that despite the fact that divorce produced feelings of anger, loss, and pain, the usual avenues of expression were not always available; divorce, unlike other major events of life, does not have a ritual attached to it that enables those involved to express their feelings openly. Divorce is still a relatively private affair; unlike birth, marriage, or death it doesn't provide a setting in which our feelings can be communicated; it does not therefore allow those affected to act in ways that will elicit response from others, to receive an explanation of their bewilderment, comfort for their pain, someone to hold on to while being angry. So many of those we met had carried, or were still carrying, the burden imposed by the unsympathetic attitudes of those involved, particularly their parents and relatives as well as those outside the family whose attitudes to divorce made them unable to help with the children's feelings of loneliness, of being different, set apart.

Our findings in this area of help led us to conclude that many more children would have been helped, less confused, less lonely, less angry, less damaged had their parents been helped. Helped to express their feelings about what was happening to them, helped by receiving comfort and understanding, and helped to find ways of assisting their children deal with this crisis.

The children we met who felt that their parents had coped adequately with explanations, who had provided safety and security at a confusing time, whose parents had talked with them, were those who appeared to have surmounted the difficulties, who could feel sad but not despairing, could acknowledge the pain but not be crippled by it, who could get on with living without looking back and blaming. So many of those who were left to fend for themselves saw their parents' divorce, the fears that it produced, the loss of confidence they experienced, as being to blame for the lack of success in their own lives. While apparently living satisfactory lives in many ways they themselves considered that greater success or greater satisfaction could have been theirs if only they had been helped at the vital time.

Jonathan seems to be right – until such time as separating parents can be helped to help their children more effectively (or even when they can) there do need to be others. The children who had found 'others' were grateful – for their explanations, their willingness to listen, their understanding, their just being there. Pauline, who wrote poems, said, "Happiness is happiness – it expresses itself, but sadness and loneliness don't – they've got to be helped to be expressed." Pauline's poems were written with teachers in mind, one at her junior, the other at her secondary school. "These two people I owe everything to as they both in their ways helped me through the hardest periods of my understanding of what was going to happen."

## Pauline's poems

I cry, thou my tears hide not the sadness in my eyes,
And through the day I've sat and wondered,
Wondered where I should really be,
What I should really do.
Smiles hide not the sadness in my heart,
Nor soften the sorrow in my soul,
The wandering of the mind, battles against the remorseful soul,
To wash away the inbedded bitterness,
Good memories, break through like spring flowers, to be crushed by storm
   of swirling garbage,
And through the day I'll sit and smile,
People stop and look awhile,
At night when nobodies there,
I cry, though the tears hide not the sadness in my eyes.

Thanks for talking to me,
Your face and eyes,
They mean a lot to me,
More than you will ever know,
I love you,
And always remember you,
I need you,
But will never be able to tell you,
Help me, I need somebody
More you did so much more, no one least of all you will ever know,
You were me, you gave me so much to live for,
Don't go away,
I want to talk to you again,
I need you,
You were for me, you kept me, my mind safe from dying.

## Notes and suggested reading

Despite the need for help which we met in this project and despite the increasing professional knowledge and understanding about pain and uncertainty experienced by families involved in divorce, the help and services available are patchy and unclear and often confusing to the prospective user (see *Marriage Matters*, HO and DHSS Working Party HMSO 1979 for further discussion; also Finer 1974, Hooper George Allen and Unwin, 1981).

Help available today is mainly for the adults involved. This may be explained by the traditional model of working with families on the assumption that the children will eventually reap the benefit. While very young children communicated their need for parental and family help – for explanations, for comfort and reassurance, our evidence suggests that as they got older children and young people often looked elsewhere for help and when offered it could use it. We assume, therefore, given that so few young children actually received the help they needed, particularly in the area of explanation, that separating parents with young children should know where to find advice. Also there is a need for services offering help to children and young people. Recommendations about help for divorcing families and a list of some existing agencies and services together with their addresses are included in the chapter and notes 'Who Can Help and How'.

# CHAPTER 6

## CUSTODY/ACCESS

'The mother had wished to prevent the father from, as she said "so much as looking" at the child; the father's plea was that the mother's lightest touch was "simply contamination". These were the opposed principles in which Maisie was to be educated – she was to fit them together as she might.'

Henry, James (1897) *What Maisie Knew.*

When parents divorce decisions have to be made about who will continue being a full-time parent and who part-time. The child can live with only one parent at a time and the nature of contact between the child and the part-time parent becomes an important issue.

Within marriage husband and wife now have equal parental rights. Both are legal custodians of their children.[1] This continues after divorce until the courts declare otherwise and deprive one of the parents of custody while vesting all custodial rights and obligations in the other.

Ever since divorce became generally available in 1857, the courts have had the right to make orders concerning the welfare and upbringing of any children of the marriage.[2] Over fifty years ago the law first stated clearly that when decisions concerning any child in divorce proceedings are made the welfare of the child should outweigh all other considerations.[3] Today a marriage cannot be dissolved legally and a decree absolute granted unless the court is satisfied with the arrangements that have been made for the children.[4] In an overwhelming majority of cases the courts approve the arrangements which have been made by the parents without necessarily conducting detailed inquiries into these. A small proportion of cases are contested on custody issues, about six in every hundred.[5] In these cases it is the courts who decide the child's future, often taking into consideration a report by a court welfare officer (usually a probation officer designated as such and attached to a divorce court).

The decisions which are made by the parents and sometimes by the courts concern custody, care and control, access. These legal terms are often unfamiliar to adults[6] let alone children, as was found by one agency specialising in offering help to divorcing couples: The Bristol Courts Conciliation Service.

The term 'custody' is usually taken to mean the rights and obligations involved in making important decisions about the child's education, religion, health, and consent to marriage if under eighteen. Care and control means caring for the child's daily needs and creating an environment in which a child's physical, emotional and social needs can be satisfied. Access is the contact which the parent not living at home and the child have with each other. Access can be defined, or left to the parents to agree, in which case it is described as 'reasonable access'. What is reasonable is then often determined by the custodial parent. Access can be staying (when the child stays overnight or for longer) or visiting (when contact is limited to a few hours), or both.

Following separation most children (roughly eighty-five out of every hundred) stay with the mother.[7] It is usually mothers who are given custody, care and control. Joint custody orders are rare: about two out of every hundred.

In the majority of cases the legal arrangements are made by the courts end not only marriage, but the natural continuity of the parent–child relationship. One of the parents is effectively excluded from making important decisions concerning the child and has to rely on the goodwill of the custodial parent, which in many cases does not exist, to the detriment of the child. Many experts believe that joint custody orders do not work. We beg to differ and believe they could work.

The arrangements which were made for our study children reflect national trends. From the participants we learned what they mean in human terms and what were their consequences for those most directly affected: the children themselves. These were the arrangements that obtained immediately (up to six months) after the separation:

| | |
|---|---|
| Child lived with mother | 87 |
| Child lived with father | 11 |
| Child lived with grandparents | 1 |
| Child lived in a Children's Home | 1 |
| Total | 100 |

★

Two of the children knew of joint custody arrangements between their parents. The others assumed (after the meaning of the word was explained to them) that the parent with whom they lived was the 'custodial' parent. A variety of access arrangements were reported during the six months following separation and the figures below reflect the main type of access.

| | |
|---|---|
| Frequent and regular (at least once a month) | 53 |
| Infrequent and regular (at least once a month) | 11 |
| Infrequent and irregular | 14 |
| No access | 22 |
| **Total** | **100** |

Some children had staying access only, others visiting access only and some both. In some cases these arrangements changed over the course of time. Many children lost touch with the non-custodial parent, a few regained it. As time went on, the majority of children saw their non-custodial parent more infrequently and irregularly. The main types of access during the period extending from about six months after separation and the child's eighteenth birthday (or the time of interview if under eighteen) were:

| | |
|---|---|
| Frequent and regular access (at least once a month) | 36 |
| Infrequent and regular (less than once a month) | 17 |
| Infrequent and irregular | 20 |
| No access | 27 |
| **Total** | **100** |

Not many children (only about a quarter of the sample) remembered their parents making friendly arrangements. Many more remembered access being given grudgingly, the parents making it obvious that they found the granting of access difficult to tolerate. In some cases it was the child who refused to see a parent. Less than one-third of all the children remembered being involved in decisions about access. Some children were not even told what was going to happen, let alone asked for their views. Children varied in their expressed desire to participate in making decisions about access. Those who strongly disapproved of not being asked were children who were unhappy with access arrangements. About half of the children were reasonably satisfied with the arrangements while one-fifth were extremely unhappy with them.

There was a complex relationship between satisfaction and both the child's and the parents' attitude to access. There was no clear-cut relationship between satisfaction and the type of access, though younger children had a preference for frequency of contact while older ones preferred flexibility so that access could fit in with their social life and other commitments.

"I think I should see my parents equally and spend one month with my dad and one month with my mum ..." said Mike aged nine. And why not, if Mike sees this as the best arrangement for him? Liz, however, who is twelve, doesn't want to see her mother, and Doreen, eleven, doesn't want to see her father; should all these children be allowed to decide for themselves? Are they making decisions for always or will they change their minds next week, next month ... next year ...? In the present climate when the rights of children are gaining attention, this whole issue of what a child's life should be like when its parents divorce is a controversial one, and one where the wishes of children may diverge from those of their parents. Few adults believe that children should have the final say when it comes to deciding issues of custody, care, control and access, and from our experience few children believe that they should either, but many believed that their views should at least be listened to and their wishes considered. Over recent years advice and guidance from 'experts' has been conflicting. What is clear from our project is that parental separation and the practical arrangements made for parent–child contact afterwards bring about a change in parent–child relationships. From our discussions with those who know this from experience one can appreciate the strength of the feelings that surround a child's desire to have some say in, even some control over, his future relationship with his parents.

Adults, on the whole, assume that a child will love both of his parents and will want to share his life with them both as he is growing up within his parents' marriage. Come separation or divorce, however, this acceptance wavers and sometimes can shift to an entirely opposite position, even to that of believing that severing the relationship between a child and one of his parents is the best course – as if physically living apart from someone whom you know belongs to you, who cares for you and loves you, actually changes your feelings about them and their feelings about you.

Parents, because of the pain they themselves are feeling about the end of their marriage, sometimes expect those closest to them to feel the same way. But it can never be quite the same for the onlookers as for the participants, however much they appear to side with you; the children of divorced parents are onlookers. However, because they are children they are impressionable and their fear and confusion at such a time perhaps makes them more so. Parents are therefore in a powerful position to influence their children's thinking and their understanding of a confusing situation – whether they intend to do so or not – and of tipping the balance in their own favour when trying to explain what has happened and why. A state of balance is not easy for anyone to achieve, let alone to maintain for long, and children are no exception. If one is being pulled in one direction, or even both directions at once, coming down on one side is probably the most common solution. Courts dealing with divorce tend to hold a similar view.[10] They often see the answer to this tricky problem in terms of 'packaging' a child – custody, care and control to one parent – with "reasonable" access to the other, thereby depriving one parent of his or her parental rights, lessening their importance in the child's life, and rarely if ever being able to see it from Mike's point of view (one month with each parent).

Parents are parents, married or divorced; it is the child's right to have and to hold on to and to continue to share their lives with fully. Our findings do not support the view that children want to sever the relationship with a loving parent following separation and divorce. Children are clearly adept at adjusting to changed circumstances, and changes in relationships may well occur following separation; what is not easy is the experience of having changes take place all around you, yet having no voice because you are a child, no power to make sure these changes are including you and your needs.

Mike, who is quoted at the beginning of this chapter, clearly typifies the feelings of a child who loves and feels himself to be loved and wanted by both of his parents. The arrangement he describes is one that some separated or divorced parents have been able to make, but is not one that we met in our study. Liz, who doesn't want to see her mother, shared with us her doubts about whether her mother really cared for her, and whether she really wanted to continue seeing Liz. Her mother had remarried and now has a child that Liz has never seen. Some of her doubts however belong to the time before her parents were separated, and her earlier relationship with her mother. Liz also sensed her mother's difficulty in being the non-custodial parent, her uneasiness when Liz visited her, her need to keep bringing Liz presents. We don't know how much help Liz and her mother received in working out a new relationship nor how far Liz was influenced by her father's attitude towards his former wife.

Doreen, who doesn't see and doesn't want to see her father, describes her feelings on realizing that her parents' marriage was over – she cried because she wouldn't have a daddy any more. Her father did not keep contact with her, for a reason Doreen did not know. Doreen felt rejected by him and when we met her she was quite clear that her father hadn't bothered about her, hadn't cared enough for her to stay in contact and therefore she was rejecting him. We do not know why Doreen's father behaved as he did or again what help he had in understanding Doreen's feelings, but inevitably Doreen was hurt and was now striking back. What we do know, however, because Doreen told us, is that she was very upset about not having been involved at all in the arrangements that were made following her parents' separation and said she thought she ought to have been asked about continuing to see her father and would then have agreed to meet him – but not now.

Do these angry feelings last for ever? We found that generally they did not. Growing up and the passing of time make a difference; but sometimes, sadly, this comes too late for a change of heart to lead to a repairing of broken bonds. Parents grow older too and die and then remorse sets in. It was from talking with the grown-up children we met that we learned what can happen. Some of the saddest feelings came from adults who for a variety of reasons had lost a parent for ever.

Lucy was fourteen when her parents separated; they divorced two years later. She recalls being very close to her father. Following the separation Lucy lived with her mother who refused to let Lucy have anything to do with her father. He was not allowed to come to the house, as her mother put it, "to darken our doorstep". The marriage had been a stormy one and frightening for Lucy. She recalls feelings of great relief when the marriage ended. Lucy never saw her father again although the antagonism towards him was continued in his absence by Lucy's mother. Lucy was in her early twenties when she heard of her father's death. "My first feeling was one of relief because I thought 'it's ended'. Then I fell to pieces, I was crying, crying, crying. I had very vivid dreams for a long long time and especially when my son was little. I still have them, I used to think if only I could have had my father to stay we could have got to know each other, and how nice it would have been for my husband to meet him – they have much in common. I always wake up from these dreams crying. I could have contacted my father when he was alive. When I was twenty-one he put a 'Happy Birthday' greeting in the local paper. But I always felt that I had to be loyal to my mother. I felt very responsible for her."

Ken helps us see that when contact is resumed after a long gap at a different stage in one's life there is still the pain of having to face the loss that has occurred and the regrets for what might have been. Ken is in his forties and was about seven when he lost contact with his father. He recalls having had a very special relationship with him "as if we were on the same wavelength." He missed his father very much and wanted to see him, but, like Lucy, didn't want to upset his mother by going against her wishes. Ken remembers trying to find out about his father as he grew older. What sort of person he was, what were his likes and dislikes, his interests and hobbies – but Ken got little help in his attempts to picture him. Ken eventually met his father again when he was twenty-one and has continued to have occasional contact with him, but he still has to live with the sadness and the vacuum that the separation produced and which will never be filled. Ken said, "I do know that as I was growing up I was looking for a father – I still am in a way."

Another group of adults we met whose lives had been changed – sometimes dramatically – by the loss of a parent were those whose anger and blame turned on to the parent caring for them rather than on to the absent parent. These were the people who were not happy living either with their custodial parent or their step-parent and who thought the grass was greener on the other side. They idealized the absent parent – for a time at least – and the absent parent became in their minds the good parent, the parent they wanted to be with. Grace, whose parents separated when she was five, did not see her mother again until she was thirteen. Grace idealized the memory of her mother during these years. She was particularly unhappy in her relationship with her stepmother so when her own mother came back into her life Grace leapt at the opportunity to spend a lot of time in her company. She enjoyed her mother's wealth and hospitality, her very different life-style from Grace's father and stepmother. Gradually, however, as Grace grew up she began to see the other side of her mother's personality – her selfishness, her lack of care and concern for others; eventually Grace came to despise her mother as she realized she had never really cared for her, never really wanted her. "I grew to despise my mother for her rejection of me and my father – I disliked everything in myself that I dislike in my mother."

Paula never lived with her father: her parents separated before she was born and she was brought up by her mother and stepfather. Paula was reasonably secure and well provided for but said that she never fully accepted her stepfather and certainly did not share her mother's values and way of life, dictated as it was by cleanliness, tidiness, a good appearance for the neighbours' sake; Paula's mother was a rather remote, cold, unemotional person. Paula's father was completely different. "Exotic, erratic, totally unpredictable, but glamorous." Although the mother portrayed him as the bad one this had no effect upon Paula's view of him – she idealized him and held on to the feeling that he would turn out to be the good one. Paula's father used to visit her – "out of the blue when it suited him." and Paula would be thrilled. "It was his absence that made him so important," Paula said, "if he had been around more I would probably have faced the reality." Because as she grew up Paula began to see her father for what he was – a very unhappy unsettled person who had "made a mess of his life, someone to be pitied rather than idealized." Paula began to worry about herself as she faced this reality and as she experienced the pain of an unhappy first marriage and divorce followed by another marriage which also proved to be a mistake, and she worried that she might have inherited her father's philandering personality. Only now in her mid-thirties does Paula feel confident that she is in fact a separate person; she is herself and no longer fears that she will end up unhappy like her father – but Paula said, "What a lot of worrying and unhappiness I had to experience to arrive at this point!"

It does not have to be like this. Parents who separate still have to cope with their painful, angry feelings, their fears about loss and loneliness, as do their children, but separation and divorce do not necessarily have to sadden people for a large part or even the rest of their lives, or damage or cripple them. We met those for whom their parents' divorce, while bringing losses, also brought gains, and in some cases these even outweighed the losses. Those we met who had had this experience were those who had 'kept' both of their parents during and after the process of the separation, the divorce, parents' remarriage and beyond. In addition these were the people who were satisfied with the arrangements made for them, or in some cases, with them, for continuing flexible contact with both parents. Yes, they said, parental divorce brings about changes, but not always for the worse. One of the things that changed, they told us, was that "parents became nicer people." Fathers who had been morose, uninvolved, and bad-tempered, became happy, caring, enjoyable, active fathers following divorce. Mothers who had been depressed, angry, and impatient became loving, caring, coping mothers. Fiona and Valerie had this experience. Their parents had divorced two years before when the girls were seven and ten. Valerie, now twelve, told us, "We wanted to live with our mother, but I said only if this meant we could see our Dad, we didn't see much of him anyway because of his work so it was natural that we should choose to be with Mum. But now we stay with Dad at weekends. He started off by giving us treats, taking us out to places, but not now – it's his company that matters, not just the things you do. I'm happy with the arrangements and probably see more of my Dad than I do of my Mum almost, because of all the evening activities I'm involved in. Although I can still get upset about them separating it's better now, for them as well, they were not happy together so it's better being on your own with one or on your own with the other – I haven't lost anything!"

Tina and Vicky are twelve and fourteen. Their parents separated four years ago; they chose to stay with their mother. They stay with their father most weekends and go on holiday with him; they also have a flexible arrangement for seeing him at other times during the week. Vicky remembers her father during the years of the marriage as someone who couldn't show his feelings. In retrospect she thinks he was probably depressed. "He's much closer to me and Tina now," Vicky told us, "he's much more fun to be with, he's nice now and smiles more. Mum is happier too."

Anthony's father is a busy professional man who during the marriage spent a lot of time at his work and often came home late in the evening when Anthony was in bed. Anthony's parents divorced when he was seven; he is now fourteen. He sees his father each weekend and on some weekdays after school. If their mother is going out Anthony and his brother stay with their father and he also takes them on holiday. Father has remarried and has children from this marriage. Anthony and his brother feel close to their father and they see far more of him now than when he lived at home. They are happy with their arrangement. These are children whose parents obviously live within a reasonable distance of each other and this helps to provide flexibility and easy access. But what of those whose parents live at a distance? We met some children whose non-custodial parent lived and worked abroad. This does not, it seems, have to be a reason for losing or rejecting or even idealizing a parent. Alan and Gordon's father lives abroad and they can only stay with him during the school holidays. They both miss him, but they enjoy these holidays and talked about some of the compensations the arrangement brings, providing as it does opportunities to visit different, often exciting, places they would otherwise not have had the chance to see.

The certainty of being loved, despite the distance there may be between parents and children, the reaffirmation of this love by letters, telephone calls, holiday contacts, the certainty that the child is not pushed aside or replaced by step siblings, the knowledge that a space is especially the child's within the parents affections, are reassurances that the relationship and it will bring feelings of sadness, but we discovered from talking to children in this situation that parents remain as important as ever. If children do not have the reassurance and confirmation that they are loved, like Liz and Doreen they will lose hope and might even for a time lose their feelings of love. We glimpsed some of this happening when we met Desmond and Debbie. They are both angry with their father because he will not tell them where he lives. They know he lives with someone who has left her children and they don't approve! But it was their father's unreliable, erratic behaviour that made them most angry – he lets them down, not coming to see them when he says he will. "He just pleases himself and doesn't care about us – we don't want to see him any more," they told us. Desmond and Debbie clearly don't feel their father has kept a special place for them in his affections.

Change and adjustment are issues to be dealt with both by the adults and the children involved in the process of divorce. Our conversations reveal that people of whatever age will cope with such issues for good or ill, but if it is a good early outcome that is being aimed at, parents who are divorcing need to continue to fulfil their functions and their responsibility as parents – or sometimes will need help in doing so, because their children clearly do not see divorce as a process which has to separate them from either of their parents. They see it for what it is: a process that separates or releases the parents from one another. It is also clear that a child's 'natural' view of divorce can be changed by fear and insecurity, or by persuasion, or even by indoctrination by one parent, and can thereby for a time at least appear to have resolved the balancing position by opting for one side against another – but with such regret and remorse later on that the cost seems too high.

Adults are sometimes, it appears, in danger of making assumptions, whether on the basis of certain views held by 'experts' or by society, or by what the ex-marital partner says or perhaps by misunderstanding the behaviour and the feelings of their children at such a stressful time as parental separation – we don't know.

From our conversations with those who had been involved in having some say in access and custody arrangements we must conclude that assumptions are to be avoided at all costs and that they are no substitute for communication. Children can face the reality of separation, they can face the reality that because of separation their lives will be changed, and, as we have seen, it may well be for the better. What they find difficult, feel angry and upset about, become rejecting and unloving about, is the loss of someone who is still in reality available to them, by that person removing themselves from the child's life, or by not keeping that special place available for them. Maybe they assume that their ex-spouse's view of them will of necessity be shared by their children, or perhaps because of the most common adult fault – that of assuming that children will not have sensible views about how their lives should be ordered – they fail to include their children when taking decisions and making plans for the separated family's future.

George, who is nine, had something to say about assumptions. George was six when his parents separated; although it had been an unhappy marriage and George remembers it as sometimes violent, he was greatly shocked on hearing (or rather overhearing) that the marriage was over. "No one told us – they should have told us what was happening instead of me just listening in." No one asked George what he wanted after the parents' decision to separate been had taken. Nothing worked out as he had hoped it would, no one talked about plans. He lives with his mother, but wants to live with his father; he has not been able to tell either of his parents how he feels or what he wants or how unhappy he is. He remembers crying for weeks, alone in bed at night and at school. He thinks about it all the time, he told us, and has no one to talk to about his feelings. During the time the interviewers spent with George it became obvious that he was a very depressed boy, trapped by his mothers' assumptions. It would seem that satisfactory access arrangements cannot be packaged according to a clearly prescribed formula. What suits one child and his parents may not be suitable in another case. There are some practical considerations, such as travelling and its cost. Of paramount importance are the attitudes of all those involved: parents, children, the courts and such people as teachers who may be confronted by the child's parents and step-parents simultaneously.

Access is a way of implementing the continuity of the parent–child relationship. In some cases access may, of course, be detrimental, but these circumstances appeared to be rare.

## Satisfaction with post-divorce custody and access arrangements

| Degree of satisfaction | Number |
| --- | --- |
| Very dissatisfied | 6 |
| Dissatisfied | 14 |
| Average | 12 |
| Satisfied | 22 |
| Very satisfied | 46 |
| Total | 100 |

## Relationships with parents after separation

| Description | Mother | Father |
| --- | --- | --- |
| Bad | 23 | 27 |
| Average | 46 | 52 |
| Good | 24 | 16 |
| Changeable | 5 | 4 |
| Did not apply | 2 | 1 |
| Total | 100 | 100 |

## Notes and suggested reading

1. The Guardianship Act, 1973, gave parents equal rights. Until then the father was presumed to be the legal guardian of the child.
2. Matrimonial Causes Act, 1857.
3. The Guardianship of Infants Act, 1925, laid down the principle of the welfare of the child being paramount in decisions concerning the child.
4. The Matrimonial Proceedings (Children) Act, 1958, laid down that a court must be satisfied with the arrangements made for any children of the family before the marriage can be dissolved.
5. Parkinson L. "Joint Custody," *One Parent Times*, No.7, NCOPF October, 1981.
6. Ibid.
7. This figure is based on two studies of custody orders:
   Maidment, S., *A Study in Child Custody*, Part I Family Law Vol. 6(7) 1976, pp. 195-200

Eekelar, J. and Clive, E (1977): *Custody After Divorce: The Disposition of Custody in Divorce Cases in Great Britain*. Centre for Socio-Legal Studies, Wolfson College, Oxford.

8. Parkinson, L. op.cit.
9. Contrast for example Goldstein, J., Freud, A., and Solnit, A. J. (1973): *Beyond the Best Interests of the Child*. Collier MacMillan, London, with Wallenstein, J. and Kelly, J. (1980): *Surviving the Breakup*. Basic Books USA.
10. Eekelar, J. and Clive, E. op. cit. Maidment, S. op. cit.
11. For further discussion of joint custody see:
    Nerls, N, and Morgenbesser, M. (1980): Joint Custody: An Exploration of the Issue, *Family Process* 19, pp. 117–125
    Haddad, R. M. (1978): '*The Disposable Parent*' *The Case for Joint Custody*, New York, Penguin Books.
    Galper, M. (1978): *Co-Parenting (Sharing Your Child Equally)*. Philadelphia Running Press.

# CHAPTER 7

# COUNTING PENNIES

'There was an old woman who lived in a shoe;
She had so many children she didn't know what to do,
She gave them some broth without any bread ...'

We have deliberately left out: 'And whipped them all soundly and put them to bed' so as not to imply a connection between poverty and bad parenting although living on a shoestring does make parenting difficult.

Our main reason for inquiring into children's reactions and views on their material circumstances was the knowledge that following separation many families experience a considerable drop in their standard of living. Many live in poverty. Financial difficulties cause parents a great deal of stress. We wondered how children experienced their material circumstances and if they felt and reacted in the ways in which adults often expect them to do.

There is a clear and direct link between an increase in the number of divorces[1] and an increase in the number of one-parent families[2]. Following separation, children continue to live with only one parent, though for some this may only be for a time as many divorced parents remarry.[3,4]

One-parent families are among the poorest sections of our society alongside other groups such as old age pensioners, the unemployed, and physically disabled people. One-parent families are poor and worse off than two-parent families for a number of reasons: a high proportion of married women, especially once the children are at school, go out to work. This means that in a two-parent family there are two incomes to support the children instead of one. Even when there is only one income in a two-parent family it is usually that of the man, whereas the great majority of one-parent families are headed by women[5] whose income is lower than that of the man. In April 1980 the average gross weekly income of male and female employees was £121.50 and £78.80 respectively, the average gross income of a woman being £42.70 lower than that of a man.[6]

There is an assumption behind public policy that the male head of the household is responsible for supporting the rest of the family. This is also true of the welfare state. This assumption has resulted in women being in some way disadvantaged. Men are paid more than women. A single woman with children may find it hard to find employment and considered to be a poor bet. "Who is going to look after the children when they are ill?" is a question often asked at interviews for jobs. Many married women give up their work and interrupt their careers to look after their home and family then find it difficult to re-enter the labour market when the marriage has broken up.

A much higher proportion of one-parent than two-parent families live on social security;[7] this means living at subsistence level of rent, food, and fuel, with no money left for new clothes, holidays and outings or even tea or coffee to offer one's friends, making social life difficult.

Contrary to what is a common myth, maintenance plays only a minor role. There are no official up-to-date statistics, but there are some figures which indicate that only a minute proportion of women with children rely on maintenance partly or wholly as their main source of income. A major government survey in 1974 revealed that over 50 percent of maintenance orders made by magistrates' courts were in arrears.[8] A recent small survey conducted among fifty women eligible for maintenance found that only seven were receiving it – the amounts being extremely low.[9] The reasons for this are complex. The main one seems to be that very few men earn enough money to support two households. There are also other reasons: whereas many men would be willing to support their children they may also, under the present legislation[10] (which is under review) be expected (quite unrealistically) to support the ex-wife. Many men resent this and either temporarily give up work or do not declare their true earnings. Many mothers do not like to pursue their ex-husbands for reasons of pride, exasperation, or fear of upsetting access arrangements which are going well. Maintenance would not improve the circumstances of those on social security, as it would be deducted from their allowance.

Housing is another area in which one-parent families are disadvantaged compared with two-parent families. Proportionately fewer are owner-occupiers, more live in poor accommodation with fewer amenities. This means shared bathrooms and toilets, fewer children having a bedroom or even a bed and a place in which to study to themselves.[11]

A major study[12] comes to the conclusion that if children from one-parent families do not do as well at school and leave school earlier than children from two-parent families, this is due to being financially disadvantaged, not in itself to having a broken home.

Parents who bring up their children without enough money worry about daily necessities. They often go without themselves to make sure that the children are reasonably well fed. Parents worry when they have to deprive their children of clothes and outings and all sorts of things available to those from better-off families. Some parents find it very hard to refuse a child's request for money or treats, not wishing to deprive their child or for fear of losing the child's love.

Many single parents prefer to work rather than to rely on social security or maintenance. This brings with it new worries: suitable arrangements have to be made for the daily care of pre-school-aged children. They will have to be looked after by relatives, friends, in day nurseries (where there is a shortage of places) and by daily 'minders' who should be approved and registered by a local authority. A young school-aged child may have to be collected from school and looked after during the holidays. Working hours and travelling distance have to take account of all this and a child's illness may necessitate prolonged absence from work and pleas for the employer's sympathetic cooperation. Working overtime to bring in extra money becomes impossible.

It is sometimes easier for the non-custodial parent to lavish money and gifts on the child than for the custodial parent to provide daily needs. In these circumstances, there is often anger, resentment, and mutual accusation of being unreasonable. The non-custodial parent may feel he or she wishes to compensate the child for absence and fears losing the child's love. The custodial parent may not wish to be unfavourably compared with the absent parent and be seen as the one who deprives the child. A parent who is worried about money and feels unhappy and insecure may wonder if the child is picking up this atmosphere. Parents wonder about the extent to which children resent being deprived. A worried parent may not be available to the child emotionally, to play with them, to do things together or listen attentively to a young child's account of his or her school day, or an adolescent outburst about the latest crisis. Worries about day-to-day existence consume a great deal of physical and mental energy.

It is not always the custodial parent who has money worries. Few can afford to run two households and the non-custodial parent finds him or herself deprived of the family home, moving into inferior accommodation, following a separation which they may not have chosen.

Once there is enough money for necessities, adults differ in how they choose to spend or save. A great deal is known about how adults spend money and their attitudes to material things, far less about children's views and priorities. It was these that we chose to explore. We wondered how children perceived their material circumstances and any changes in them; we wondered to what extent these perceptions were related to real changes and circumstances. Did children worry about the same things as adults, what were their priorities and what was important to them? What factors influenced these perceptions and priorities? Was age, for instance, of vital importance? These were some of the questions we asked.

When talking about material circumstances a variety of things were mentioned by our volunteers, some relating to one or both parents and others more directly to the child. We were told about parents' occupations and given overall impressions of how well or badly off the family was; significant change in either direction; discrepancies in parents' income; parents' attitude to money and spending habits. Housing and moves were considered important. Comparisons were made with school friends, relatives, and parents' friends. We were told about clothes, pocket-money, treats, holidays, and outings. Pets and hobbies were also mentioned. Feelings towards parents and their partners were often expressed alongside accounts of material things.

Volunteers' assessment of financial effects of separation were as follows:

| | |
|---|---|
| 41 children | were "worse off" |
| 19 children | were "better off" |
| 30 children | were "about the same" |
| 10 children | were "not sure" |

Total 100

Did children's assessments correspond with reality and, if so, to what extent? Although we had no means of testing this, we were made aware of the discrepancies between perceptions and what might have been reality by what the children themselves told us. It was these discrepancies which helped us to appreciate the importance of attitudes, feelings and individual priorities.

The discrepancy between real and perceived circumstances is well illustrated by the accounts given by three sisters, Rita, Marilyn and Yvonne who were respectively seventeen, twelve and eight when their parents parted on fairly amicable terms. Whereas Rita does not remember being particularly upset it was Yvonne, the youngest, who remembers missing her father terribly, even though she saw him often, and crying at the window for a long time after waving good-bye to him after each of his visits. Financially, the family have always been reasonably well off; the father is a personnel officer and the mother works as a receptionist.

The perceptions of these three sisters were totally different, as illustrated by their comments:

Rita reported an improvement:

> I remember that I was lavished with things. I remember that specially because both of them [parents] gave me more than I had before, both of them gave me more material things. I remember getting twice as many presents, twice as many sweets, and in my mind this was a good thing.

Marilyn reported no change:

> Things were about the same, we still had our treats and holidays, nothing much changed, they still played cards and chess together.

Yvonne reported a big change for the worse:

> We could no longer afford treats and holidays, money was short, everything changed.

It was Yvonne who was the most unhappy of the three sisters and we can only conclude that her unhappiness coloured her perceptions about money. Rita, the eldest, was ready shortly to move out of the family and was therefore least affected and unhappy. This allowed her to enjoy the treats and presents she received which she saw as her parents' way of compensating her for the break-up. She also felt was something glamorous about having divorced parents.

How children saw and described their material circumstances was affected by a variety of factors, and feelings were important. For those who were unhappy and missed a parent these feelings tended to colour the view of the financial situation. They were more likely to notice changes for the worse, or even believe that such changes had taken place even when they had not.

On the other hand, if as a result of separation things had improved, for instance, if there was less tension or the child had been very angry with the parent who left home, the child was more likely to report an improvement. Feeling coloured their perceptions: if other things had improved, then the financial situation also was seen through rosy spectacles.

An example of this effect is Debbie, aged fourteen, who expressed strong feelings of anger, typical of many adolescents, towards her father, who left her mother for another woman and had rejected Debbie ever since she was a little girl. Debbie considers her father's departure "good riddance" and sees a great improvement in the family's financial arrangements due to what she considers her mother's great generosity and her father's meanness.

There were children whose financial situation did improve or remain the same and objectively they could see that this was so. Yet, they missed their absent parent and certain things that were provided by him or her. There were times when they felt sad and thought that materially they were worse off than before. Many different kinds of things were valued; an adult might consider some of them insignificant. They ranged from father's toolbox to bags of sweets and crisps. To children these things were important and coloured their assessment of the effect of separation on their material wellbeing.

One of the children who brings home to us the importance of small gifts and their subjective and symbolic meaning is Cindy, aged fourteen. Her parents had lived apart for seven years. She still misses the bags of sweets and crisps that her father used to leave on her bed when he came home late at night for Cindy to find in the morning. Cindy's mother, a professional woman, is well off and Cindy has not suffered any material deprivation since divorce. Cindy appreciates nice clothes and good holidays, but attaches as much importance to less expensive gifts. There are times when she feels she is less well off since separation, even though she knows that she is not really. Her feelings about her father's small gifts are as important as objective facts about her mother's salary and her pocket-money.

Since we had no way of objectively measuring changes in the children's financial circumstances, we were guided by what is generally known about the adverse effects of divorce on finances. We accepted that how children saw and felt about these changes had its own validity.

We learned what it was like for the children who saw themselves as poorer following separation. For many children being poor meant being deprived of things like expensive food and other things they had previously taken for granted. Fruit became a luxury, only the cheapest vegetables were bought. Buying tea, coffee and soft drinks for the child to offer to friends became a problem. Pennies had to be watched. There were children who could never go and choose new clothes. They had to wear what was handed down or bought at jumble sales. Teenagers, especially, resented this, but younger children also preferred new clothes to old and some were so poor as to have to wear second-hand socks.

Outings, presents and treats had to be cut. When these did happen they could not always be fully enjoyed as children knew that money was short and they or the parent might have to go without something else.

Many children, specially only and eldest ones, worried about how a single parent was managing and wanted to help; not being able to led to feelings of uselessness and frustration. Anger was generated when the absent parent was seen to be better off than the one who had to care for the child and had a daily struggle to keep going. Sometimes big changes for the worse were noticed, but there were also circumstances in which there had been no change since the divorce and still the child was angry. Some absent parents had done well financially and the child was aware that he or she was not benefiting from this improvement.

One of the adults who vividly described for us what it was like to be poor following separation was Maureen. Maureen, aged thirty-eight and now happily married with two children, was eight when her father left the family and went to live with another woman. Maureen's mother got a job in a library in a nearby town; she had not worked previously and would not have done so by choice. Her salary was very low.

> There was a maintenance order; the money came ... but it was always late. It [the separation] made a tremendous difference to our standard of life, all of us counted the pennies ... I remember going into a greengrocer's to buy some tomatoes. There were two kinds and I asked for the cheaper ones. When I realized I had been sold the more expensive ones I was really angry.

Maureen still remembers her surprise at the strength of her anger on that occasion. She also remembers feeling ashamed and comparing herself unfavourably with other people.

> We had other people's cast-offs. We were very much the poor relations, both compared with my father's and my mother's brother's family. Our home was dowdy and shabby compared with theirs.

Maureen knew that her mother was worried about money; later on she discovered the full extent of the difficulties and was grateful to her mother for trying to cover up her troubles and to protect Maureen. As the eldest of three children, she wished she could help her mother in some way and felt helpless because there was nothing she could do. She loved her mother and developed a very negative attitude to her father, blaming him for deserting the family for another woman. She does not remember missing him. In retrospect, she feels she coped by taking entirely her mother's side. She interpreted her father's irregular, low maintenance payments as meanness and irresponsibility. She missed family outings in his car – her mother could hardly even afford public transport to get to work and often walked part of the way.

During the most difficult time the landlady was extremely helpful, often patiently waiting for overdue rent and telling the mother not to worry. The family eventually moved to another town to be near the mother's relatives. Their uncle owned a house and a greengrocer's shop. They lived rent free and could buy such luxuries as fruit at a price they could afford. The help of the landlady and the mother's extended family made a great difference to the financial situation and although Maureen knew about the financial difficulties she seems to have found out the position for herself rather than through any complaints by her mother.

Following separation many parents had had to move with their children to different accommodation. Sometimes it was seen from the child's point of view as running away from the family home. Sometimes the parent with the child just stayed on in the family home, but later had to find somewhere else to live. Moves were usually to accommodation which was seen by the child as inferior and sometimes there was more than one move. Children commented on more cramped conditions, the flat or the house not being as nice as the one in which they lived before and compared the furniture unfavourably. In far fewer cases were the moves to better accommodation or to that of a comparable standard.

Where and how they lived mattered to children. It was important to them to have their own bedroom – a place where they could be alone with their friends, to keep their toys or hang up their posters, according to age and individual choice. Children felt deprived, sad, and angry when their housing conditions deteriorated as a result of separation.

Being aware of adverse changes in financial circumstances and the feelings and reaction to this awareness need to be considered separately. Not all children were equally upset and some do not remember being upset by money matters at all. Some attitudes and circumstances aggravated poverty, others cushioned the impact.

There were a number of factors which seemed to turn awareness of poverty into great unhappiness for the child. Some parents shared their worries more than freely with very young children and this was resented, either at the time or subsequently. Children felt that it was unfair for a parent to lean on the child too heavily and that such worries should have been shared with other adults: relatives and friends.

We were told by Joan, a twenty-five-year-old student, whose parents separated when she was five:

> I was always very much aware that money was short. My mother complained and talked to me about money at a much earlier age than other parents would have done, about the financial worries that she had. She would talk to me more than she talked to my grandmother. She would say, 'You cannot have this or that because you have not got a father'.

Joan remembers herself as an unhappy child with a chip on her shoulder. She was and still is angry with both her parents for involving her in their financial difficulties and their post-divorce battles.

A number of parents, such as Joan's, involved their children in their financial battles. They took great pains to point out to the child that they were worse off as a result of the absent parent's meanness and irresponsibility and that such a parent would not behave as they did if they really cared for the child. Children often took sides and so coped with divided loyalties. Telling a child that a parent was mean seemed to be a concrete way of demonstrating that he or she was a bad person. Young children seemed to accept this without much questioning; such accusations added fuel to the fire for angry older children. Later, older children and adults looked back with sadness and resentment.

Children were also made very unhappy by thinking that the parents were spending money on themselves or a new partner, to win their love or approval. Such children felt not only poorer, but left out and neglected.

It was especially in adolescence that poverty brought feelings of shame and resentment. It is well known that teenagers are very conscious of their appearance and their clothes. This is true of both boys and girls. Clothes are an outward symbol of conformity, of being like one's peers, not stepping out of line. The approval of one's appearance by the peer group seems all-important, whatever parents may think of the latest fashion. It is not only teenagers, however, who are clothes-conscious. We all know the joy a new outfit can bring to a little girl or boy. While the young child or adolescent is still not very sure of their identity, clothes are part of it and anything that makes the child different, such as a derogatory remark from another child or adult, can arouse a great deal of shame, embarrassment and self-doubt. Many children told us how selfconscious they felt when they compared themselves unfavourably with their peers or when others commented on their clothes. Adverse and derogatory comments made by others, especially people who were important to the child or young person, could make them feel acutely ashamed and embarrassed.

The feelings of adolescents, their need for conformity and being cared for, are illustrated by Mark. Mark, a twenty-one-year-old student, was eight when his mother left home. His father was shattered and began to drink heavily. "In no way were we poor ... it [the separation] made me as a person worse off." What did change was his father's attitude: Mark became a convenient scapegoat for his father's anger and resentment and Mark was blamed for things which were not his fault. While Father bought himself a new car and new suits and entertained his girlfriend expensively, Mark grew out of his clothes. "My jackets always seemed too short and had holes in them. I was conscious of my shabby appearance." To make matters worse, his teachers always seemed to be commenting on it. Mark was very unhappy generally and felt rejected by both his parents.

Children were protected from the full impact of impoverished circumstances after divorce by their parents and the environment. There were many children who were aware that money was short, but do not remember being particularly worried about it.

After separation some mothers went out to work or began to work full-time rather than part-time. The children remembered their mothers working hard for long hours. If the mother seemed to be happy and coping well, the child did not resent being denied various things. Some children were proud of their mothers who returned to work or full-time study after separation, even if this meant financial sacrifices. What seemed important to the child was how the parent was managing and whether they were enjoying what they were doing or considered it a burden.

The environment could also cushion the child against poverty. Having good neighbours or relatives, feeling that the single parent was getting support, was important. It was the children who compared their situation unfavourably with other adults who felt 'different'. Those whose neighbours and schoolmates were not better off than they had no reason to feel different. One of the children whose family was poorer after separation was Diane, yet poverty had little impact on her. Diane, a twenty-four-year-old student, whose parents separated when she was six, was born in the East End of London. "My earliest memories are of cops chasing boys over rooftops ...

Financially, we were always hard up, even more so after they split up."
Diane's father was an unskilled labourer and after the separation her mother
worked as an indoor dress machinist, earning very little. After separation
her father tried to support two families on his low wage; himself and his
girlfriend and Diane and her mother. Diane remembers her mother at the
sewing machine, whenever she came home from school and early in the
morning.

After separation, Diane saw her father "every Friday down the bottom of
the road. It was goodies time." Father would buy her sweets and toys.
There were also grandparents living near.

> There were goodies again, my grandmother would come down the road
> or I would walk up and she would buy me a bag of sweets. Living in that
> kind of area [East End of London] there was always someone to give you
> breakfast, or a cold drink, or what have you.

Although she remembers fights and poverty, Diane does not remember
being generally unhappy; her relatives and neighbours were obviously very
supportive and she never felt isolated. She lived in an area where many
families were poor and did not have friends who were better off with whom
to compare themselves. What children considered important differed from
child to child. Some things were considered important by all children.
These were such things as where they lived, and enough money to buy food
and decent clothes. So were outings and treats. Regular pocket-money was
greatly valued – it gives the child some control and choice. Children liked to
have their birthdays remembered and acknowledged by cards and gifts even
if only small ones. We did not come across any children who did not attach
some importance to these things.

There were also individual priorities and what was treasured and missed
by each child was also to some extent individual. Only each individual child
could tell us what mattered most to them and what was for them an
important gap. It was remembering the loss of her cat that brought tears to
Veronica's eyes during our long talk with her. Veronica, now aged
thirty-five, told us how she and her mother moved house when her parents
split up. Veronica was twelve at the time. As pets were not allowed at the
new house, Veronica had to leave her cat behind in the care of her father and
his girlfriend – neither of whom was fond of animals. The cat died some
weeks later and at the time Veronica grieved over the loss of her pet more
than she had grieved about other losses. Even though she subsequently
missed her father and did not get on particularly well with her mother,

whom she considered mean, she still considers the loss of her cat as particularly painful. It was something she never shared with her parents, not wishing to upset them.

For a number of children nothing much appeared to have changed financially following the separation. These were usually children who stayed in the same house, whose custodial parent did not have any money worries, or if they did, managed to conceal them well.

A number of children told us that, as a result of parental separation, they were better off. This seems to have been so for a number of reasons. Some children acquired new relatives through either one, or both, parents remarrying. Some acquired step-parents, who were generous, others also grandparents. There were also children who felt that one or both parents tried to compensate them for the break-up by providing material things. Often this was the parent with whom the child did not live. The position of such a parent can be a difficult one, complicated by feelings of guilt and regret. Living under the same roof with one's child and doing things together naturally is very different from trying to entertain the child and finding things to do and places to go during access periods. The non-custodial parent may spend money on the child to make up for not having two parents at home and to gain the child's affection.

Some children felt pleased by this improvement, such as Stan, aged fifteen. As a result of parental divorce he has acquired a stepmother, stepfather and two new sets of step-grandparents. He gets more presents, more pocket money, more treats than he ever did when his parents were together. Although unhappy for a time, he now seems quite content with his situation.

There were also children who were not so pleased about the fact that more gifts and money were spent on them. We were given examples of their feeling embarrassed by parents' efforts to compete with each other. Children often felt this was a way of winning their loyalty and did not feel comfortable about it. Some saw gifts and instant gratification of requests for money as parents' way of opting out of other responsibilities such as regular visits or loving the child and spending time with him. Discomfort was also experienced when buying things, and providing treats was the non-custodial parent's way of using the time of access. As one sixteen-year-old put it, "Why do we always have to do things, why does my father keep on asking, 'What shall we do next? Why can't we just be together?'"

How children view money and gifts from their parents is to a great extent coloured by their attitude. There were a number of children who on occasions, or always, refused money from a parent they felt angry with. It was usually children who had a good relationship with their parent who accepted and enjoyed things without guilt or anger. Some children demand material things from the parent they feel angry with.

One of the adolescents whose feelings affected her attitude to taking money from a parent was Shirley. Shirley, seventeen, was thirteen when her parents parted. Shirley does not like taking money from her father. "I prefer to save up for what I want. It is not as though my father can make up for what he has done." Shirley is angry with her father for leaving her family and having an affair while he was still married to Shirley's mother. Shirley has always got on excellently with her mother and since the separation has felt that she is even closer and has more respect for her. Her once-good relationship with her father has deteriorated. Although she felt sorry and concerned for him at the time of separation she now has little respect for him. She sees him fairly regularly during holidays and is aware that his standard of living is much higher than her mother's, but says she is satisfied with what her mother and she have. Shirley feels that it is better to wait for things than have everything she wants immediately, particularly if this means accepting money from her father.

Children who got on well with their parents were able to "take no for an answer". They did not feel angry or upset for long if they were refused something they had asked for, provided they were given a clear reason, which did not involve labelling the other parent as mean. Children were able to adjust and if a parent was seen to be managing well, did not mind asking for things and knew their requests would be granted if they were reasonable and the money was available.

For a time at least following separation and divorce a child is likely to live with a single parent and experience a drop in the standard of living. Parents cannot fully protect their children from the realization and impact of this change. The major remedies do not lie in the hands of individual parents and maybe this realization can make them feel less guilty and lessen the need to over-compensate the child for something that is not the parent's fault. The present State allowances which single parents can claim other than Social Security are Family Income Supplement, if the income is below certain limits, and a small additional allowance known as One-Parent Benefit (£3.65 as from November 1982).

Many single parents choose to go out to work. They need jobs in which there is no discrimination against single parents. Many hide the fact that they have children. Also needed are adequate day care facilities for children under five and some provision for schoolchildren after school hours and during holidays.

A major and possibly the only adequate large-scale remedy could be a guaranteed maintenance allowance from the State with responsibility for collecting maintenance also being vested in the State without excluding satisfactory private arrangements. The Finer Committee set up by the Government made detailed recommendations in their report in 1974, which so far have not been implemented.

Within these major limitations there is still much that parents can do to cushion the child against the impact of poverty or controversial money issues. When money is short it is tempting to blame the ex-spouse for financial hardship. Doing so in front of the child hardly helps the parent and only adds to the child's distress.

Some parents can be very demanding and use the question of money to punish the ex-spouse. Anger can also be expressed in a way hurtful to the child by rejecting or belittling what is given to the child directly or indirectly. The clothes are said to be the wrong colour or the toys not the right kind. It is the child's feelings that are hurt as much as the giver's. In the best interest of the child perhaps gifts can be accepted with a little more grace than they sometimes are.

Gifts and money, when given to the child as part of a competition between parents for its love and approval, are not likely to make the child happy in the long run, though some children use the situation temporarily to their advantage. Children appreciate what is given to them as a genuine expression of caring and love.

Above all what helps children to cope is the realization that parents have reached some agreement about money as far as the child is concerned and that they appreciate each other's position. The non-custodial parent may feel that special treats are one of the few things he or she can still provide for the child and the custodial parent need not feel any obligation to provide these continually. It is the custodial parents who usually have to deny things day-to-day. How they feel about it also calls for understanding. Money, like separation, has to be talked about.

## Notes and suggested reading

1. There was an increase in the number of divorces granted in the UK from 80,000 in 1971 to 158,000 in 1980.
   Source: Central Statistical Office, Social Trends 1982. HMSO table 2.13.

2.  At the same time there was an increase in the total number of one-parent families from 570,000 in 1971 to an estimated 950,000 in 1981. Most of the increase is accounted for by an increase in the number of divorced women, followed by separated women and a slight increase in the number of male single parents.
    Source: Annual Report 1981, One Parent Families.
3.  In 1979 33 percent of all marriages in Great Britain were remarriages for at least one of the spouses.
4.  In recent years there has also been an increase in the number of marriages in which both spouses had been married before.
    Source: Social Trends, op. cit., table 2.11.
5.  In 1979, out of a total number of 860,000 one-parent families, 760,000 were headed by women.
    Source: Annual Report 1981. op. cit.
6.  Social Trends, op. cit. table 5.6.
7.  Annual Report 1981 O.P.F. op. cit.
    58 percent of all families with children on social security are one-parent families, although only one in eight of all families in the general population are headed by a single parent.
8.  DHSS Report of the Committee on One Parent Families. OHMS 1974.
9.  *Maintenance: Putting Children First.* OPF 1981.
10. Section 25, Matrimonial Causes Act 1973.
11. Burnell and Wadsworth, J. (1982): 'Home Truths', *One Parent Times*, OPF.
12. Ferri, E., *Growing Up in a One-Parent Family*. NFER 1976. A study based on a cohort of children born in one week in 1958 known as the National Child Development Study.
13. Marsden, D. (1969): *Mothers Alone*, Allen Lane. Not all mothers on social security found it equally hard to manage.

# CHAPTER 8

## SECOND TIME AROUND

The fairy stories we read as children are laced with references to step-relations. Second wives and step-mothers frequently appear in these stories and are invariably cruel. Thus they inevitably are linked in our minds with wicked witches. We all know the story of Cinderella and her wretched life with her stepmother and stepsisters until rescued by a fairy godmother.

Snow-White's mother died and her father, the king, took a second wife 'who was very beautiful, but so proud that she could not think that anyone could surpass her'. Snow-White grew more and more beautiful and when the wicked Queen consulted her mirror she was told that she was no longer 'the fairest of them all'. The Queen ordered Snow-White to be taken away and killed 'that I may never see her more'.[1]

Iona and Peter Opie comment on the prevalence of stepmothers in fairy stories and when discussing the story of the Sleeping Beauty tell us that the King's mother turns out to be 'an ogress yearning to eat her grandchildren'– an appetite usually attributed to stepmothers.[2]

Stepfathers seem to be treated more leniently in fairy tales. We wondered if the fairy stories which children enjoy reading and being told bore any relationship to how they viewed and related to step-parents in real life. We asked them about remarriage and partners following separation and how they felt about them.

"I think I was upset because that meant the end of my hopes that Mum and Dad would get together again." Tracey was eleven years old and talking about her feelings on hearing that her father had remarried. Tracey made us think that as far as young children are concerned it is remarriage that marks the end of marriage for them rather than the separation or divorce. Perhaps Tracey is speaking for many children who hold inside themselves the hope of parental reconciliation, the hope of living happily ever after. Perhaps what Tracey says helps adults appreciate some of the dangers that lurk for some step-families where the children's hopes are shattered and the reality of not coming together again has to be faced, step-families where the adults have not appreciated the meaning of remarriage for the children.

Remarriage seemed to bring a mixture of loss and gain from a child's point of view. Some of the children we met saw it as bringing a great deal of happiness, while for others it meant sadness or even disaster. Successful remarriage, or rather successful step-relationships, appear to be linked, in part at least, to the age of the child when remarriage takes place, and as one might expect by the space between the end of one marriage and the beginning of the next.

Although we might imagine that there are different sets of feelings for children according to whether it is their custodial parent or their non-custodial parent who remarries, this did not seem to be the case. The children we met did not make clear distinctions between their parents and spoke of both parents and their new parents as having similar importance for them.

Second marriages, and therefore step-families, have become fairly commonplace; about 50 percent of those divorced in any one year remarry within five years. Of the one hundred people we interviewed thirty-six mothers had remarried and fifty-eight fathers. A few had remarried twice.

Several children had experienced a parent having a long-standing relationship, the partner frequently living within the family. Twenty-six mothers and nineteen fathers had a steady partner. Fifteen mothers and eight fathers had had several short-lived relationships.

Despite the growing number of step-families and the greater acceptance of remarriage there is a widely held assumption that living within a step-family may well produce difficulties, usually for the children, difficulties that are different from the ones faced by natural families. It may also be that the fairy stories we read as children have coloured our expectations about step-relationships. Cinderella had a stepmother and her two ugly sisters were her stepsisters – Snow-White's stepmother ordered her to be banished from her sight and stepmothers in fairy stories frequently appear as cruel and nasty and are sometimes even portrayed as witches. Stepchildren are beautiful, good and hard done by. Stepfathers seem to have escaped this sort of archetypal portrayal.

On the whole the younger the child the better the chance of their making a successful attachment to a step-parent, we found; we also found that young girls in particular seemed to do well. They were the group who were most concerned to return the family to 'normal', by which they meant a family with two adults instead of one. Doreen, who is now eleven, was six when her parents separated from a very unhappy and sometimes violent marriage, one in which Doreen was often frightened. Doreen first met the man who was to become her stepfather when she became friendly with his daughter at the after-school activities they both attended. He was divorced and had the care of his two children. Doreen and Liz became close friends and Liz's father met Doreen's mother when taking the girls to or collecting them from their outings. "I liked him," Doreen told us. "I liked them getting married. I'm glad Mum got married again. Liz and I get on well together and I'd much rather have it like this than just Mum and me."

Angela and Julie's parents divorced four years ago when the girls were six and four. They both remember being happy as a family and recall the good things they did together with their parents. They were both unhappy on being told that their parents were separating and did hope that they would get together again. They lived with their mother after the separation and saw dad regularly. They remember missing him being around, and they still do, while continuing to see him regularly. Their parents, from what both girls said, appear to have an amicable, cooperative relationship. Both of their parents remarried in the four-year interval following the divorce. Angela and Julie continue to live with their mother. They both said how happy they were with their step-parents. Each set of parents now has another child and the girls are delighted with both step-siblings. Julie told us, "I like both my dads, I don't know which dad I like the most."

Girls of twelve presented a rather different picture. They seemed to be particularly adept – or so they told us – at frightening off prospective partners where their mothers were concerned. Annette is now eighteen. When she was twelve her mother started going out socially, following a period of withdrawal after the divorce. One day Annette's mother brought home a boyfriend. "I didn't like him at the time," said Annette, "I couldn't accept him, I didn't try to get on with him." Mother has not so far remarried.

Lorraine is twelve and doesn't like any of her mother's boyfriends. "I would be upset if she got married, but I suppose it would really depend on what sort of person he was." Louise is fifteen and told us, "When I was younger I didn't like my Mum having boyfriends. I used to get very upset and annoyed because I used to like it the way it was – our Mum to ourselves. If I didn't like them I used to make them feel uncomfortable."

The strong feelings that were aroused in twelve-year-old girls about their mother's relationships with boyfriends seemed not only to be related to their fears of someone taking over their father's place or of losing their mothers, but also to the feelings that were aroused about their mother having a sexual relationship. Annette went on to tell us that "I resented the fact that he slept here and left his clothes around the place — I really hated that."

Molly, whose mother had a number of boyfriends during Molly's early adolescence, felt "disgusted when I realized these relationships included sex." It was the same for Brenda – she can remember refusing to eat the food her mother cooked, and couldn't eat in the same room as her mother when she learnt about her mother's relationships. Janet is fifteen now; when she was around eleven or twelve years old she began to realize the nature of her mother's relationship with her boyfriend. "I didn't mind her first boyfriend, it was when Mum had another boyfriend I realized that they were having an affair and that it must have been the same with the first one. Mum used to lock the bedroom door. I was so angry. I'd go into her bedroom after she had gone out and find her boyfriend in bed. There was a sleeping bag on the floor and she used to say he slept in it – I didn't believe her. I asked her to tell me the truth and she did. I felt that I had been locked out and I was so angry. I shouted at her and hit her. She took it, and afterwards we talked about it. She explained how frightened and lonely she had been after the divorce. I felt embarrassed for a while but we talked a lot about it. It's a bit difficult with the kids at school who know he's her boyfriend, but the fact that we talked about it makes it easier."

The strong feelings that were aroused in girls about their mothers' sexual relationships seemed to relate to a time in their lives when they themselves were becoming aware of their own sexuality, at the stage at which sexuality was something to be feared and rejected and its exclusivity something to be angry about.

As girls moved further into adolescence a more accepting attitude developed towards mothers and new partners. "I've changed a lot since I was eleven or twelve," Vicky (now fourteen) told us. "I said to myself, 'If she marries again I'll run away': but now I'd really like her to marry." Louise, who used to get upset and annoyed when she was younger, was able at fifteen to tell us, "I still get a bit upset about them [the boyfriends], but I wouldn't mind her remarrying now if I liked him." And Annette can look back from the age of eighteen and say, "I can now see he was O.K. really."

Boys seemed to find their mothers relationships much easier to manage. Perhaps Bob's experience gives us a clue as to why this is so, even though Bob was a young adult at the time he refers to. Bob didn't think his mother would remarry, she was so scarred by divorce. The thought of his mother on her own as she got older worried Bob a great deal. Then one day (he was twenty-three at the time), his mother brought home her future husband. Bob was delighted and thought him a most suitable person as they seemed happy together. "I felt like a father whose daughter was bringing home her new boyfriend for the first time." The burden was shed. Bob no longer felt responsible. He gets on very well with his stepfather and it has been a very happy marriage.

Bill is fourteen, and during the past five years his mother has had two important relationships. Bill was sorry for her when they each in turn ended. He hopes his mother will remarry and if so to someone he likes.

Danny is eleven, has known his future stepfather for about a year and enjoys his company. His mother is to be married in a few months' time and Danny is delighted for her; he can see how happy his mother is now. Anthony and Edward live with their mother and have always liked their mother's boyfriends and although Edward can recall slight feelings of jealousy they are both happy with their recently acquired stepfather and say they get along very well with him. Maurice is seventeen: his parents divorced when he was four. His mother met someone special when Maurice was about six and the relationship lasted until Maurice was ten years old. Maurice liked him. "He was like a father to me, he played football and cricket with me." Maurice recalls those four years as very happy ones. He remembers his mother being 'over the moon'. Maurice said the relationship provided him with a model of how fathers behave towards children. "I never felt any threat. I think my mother was very careful to choose a man who wouldn't make me feel that way. I'd be over the moon if she came in and said she was to remarry, and if she was to have a child that would be marvellous for her."

Although the picture we were given of stepfathers was in general a positive one we were told by some we interviewed about their feelings of misery and fear when relating what their lives had been like living with their mother and stepfather, of violent abusive behaviour on the part of the step-parent. One stepfather had used his dogs to control his step-children, another was physically violent towards his step-children and their mother, forcing them to leave their home and flee to a women's refuge. Helen had to be removed from her home into the care of the local authority because of her stepfather's violence; Brenda's stepfather tried to rape her and her sister.

These were the children among the group for whom we must say that remarriage brought disaster and pain, but the balance was clearly in favour of stepfathers being 'a good thing.' Stepfathers are likely to be more acceptable to young girls and to boys of any age. They are particularly welcome to boys nearing adulthood who may be troubled by a growing awareness of their roles as 'husband substitutes' and feel relief at being able to relinquish it. However, twelve and thirteen-year-old girls have most difficulty in accepting a male step-parent. Because of their new-found awareness of their sexuality, girls of this age tend to compete with their mothers. The presence of a man who may be quite close to them in age will be embarrassing, and the strict father–daughter taboos do not operate to the same extent in these circumstances. Whatever the specific difficulties which arise between children and step-parents, we found that all children should be closely involved in the new relationship.

Sexual relationships tend to be exclusive: most couples in their courtship phase are inward-looking, wrapped up in themselves and each other. Such a relationship is not easy when there are children around, and the parents in a new relationship should be sensitive to the children's feelings. The importance of this was reinforced by the reported reactions of children who had not been properly prepared for their parent's remarriage. Larry, who was at boarding-school at the time, was introduced by his father on one of his visits to a lady. Larry didn't take much notice of her. When he next saw his father at school, Father asked, "Do you remember that lady I was with on my last visit? Well, I married her." Larry said this came as a complete surprise to him. "I tried to behave appropriately, but I was just bewildered by it." Anger and distress were, however, the most common reactions to this situation. Like Alison and her sister, "He didn't tell us he was getting married, we were absolutely furious, we only found out from a friend. He could at least have told us – he didn't include us in his plans, we felt rejected."

Stepmothers do seem to have a more difficult task than stepfathers. We found strong feelings were expressed about stepmothers whether full-time, or part-time – they were either loved or hated and we found no noticeable links with the age or sex of the children concerned. Among the examples of successful child/stepmother relationships were Lorraine, fifteen, and Louise, thirteen. They have lived with their mother since their parents divorced. They told us, "We've grown to love Mary, we owe her a lot. If it wasn't for her we wouldn't get anything from our dad. She buys us clothes and things, she's like a second mother to us." Lorraine added, "I go to her when I want to talk about things. Mum gets on really well with her, they've got a good understanding." Mary and the girls' father have no children of their marriage and the girls seemed to be describing someone who was happy to share in their care and upbringing, sharing it more with their mother than with their father, perhaps.

Liz is eleven, she doesn't have any contact with her mother and does not recall much about her. She and her father lived with Grandmother when her mother left. Her father remarried when Liz was ten, to someone with a family from a first marriage. Liz liked her stepmother from the start, she gets on well with her stepbrother and sister, and is very happy to have a new mother. Daren and Tracey's father is remarried to someone they both like very much. Tracey has moved to live with her father and stepmother, as this is more convenient now she has changed schools. She spends weekends and holidays with her mother and Daren is a frequent visitor to his father's house.

Not all children have been happy with their relationship with their stepmothers. In some cases it did seem, from the children's point of view, as though some fathers had stepped from the frying pan ... and in the process had got themselves caught between two stools! Like Bill's dad: "I liked her at first," Bill, fourteen, told us, "I can't stand her now. I think she's jealous of us taking his attention, she's horrible to us. Dad finds it difficult, he's in the middle, he likes us and he likes her. I don't resent her, I don't think she took him away from us." Bill's sister, Annette, now eighteen, feels similarly. "I liked her before I realized she was Dad's girlfriend. She has two children from a previous marriage and makes it abundantly clear that they are the favourites. She keeps saying that *her* children don't want to see *their* father. We didn't keep up our visits to Dad because of her, we represent our mother and she hates us."

Danny also seems to be having difficulties with his stepmother. "I don't like her all that much, she can be nice, sometimes, but she's a bit moany. He was going to split up from her. He knows what she's like, she cries a lot. It would be better if he just lived by himself – we'd see more of him if she wasn't there, we would visit him more often. She makes him go out to do things, like going to the shops to buy her a new dress, when we are visiting. If she wants to do something Dad hasn't got much choice otherwise she sulks and cries."

Anthony and Edward feel sorry for their father too about his unfortunate remarriage, but unlike Danny they don't feel their relationship with their father suffers. Their stepmother apparently has a fierce temper and they suspect that their father is not really very happy.

Toby, although very happy for his father who has a loving and successful second marriage, has never met his stepmother although he visits his father quite frequently. His father explained to him that his wife would be embarrassed to meet him because of Toby's mother's angry and jealous attitude towards her. "When I visit, always by arrangement, she goes out before I arrive."

Lynn and Belinda lived with their father following the divorce. Lynn was seven and Belinda thirteen when he remarried. "I didn't get on with her," Lynn said. "It must have been very difficult for her because I didn't want her as a mother. I didn't want another mother. Perhaps she wanted to be the mother immediately and I didn't feel as she wanted me to feel." Belinda told us, "I resented him not for remarrying, but for marrying someone like he did. I resent the fact that he was so blind as to marry her, she just couldn't cope. It seemed that his second marriage was just a response or a rebound to having been left by our mother. My relationship with my stepmother was bad, but it also affected my relationship with my father badly too."

Any mothering role brings with it expectations of closeness and intimacy: qualities that are difficult to avoid in relationships with stepmothers, given the way most families are organized.

Fathers and stepfathers are more likely to be away from home for a large part of the day and even if this is not so they are not usually involved in the more intimate tasks of child-rearing – perhaps this is more likely to apply in the case of stepfathers. Stepmothers are less likely to be able to avoid the more intimate tasks. Given our society's strong mother–child orientation children's attitudes will fit in with widely held beliefs that mothering contains special elements for which there cannot easily be a substitute. Stepmothers are affected by these attitudes and attempts to replace the special relationship may be tinged with guilt for them – perhaps the fairy stories are right after all! Or perhaps Dorothy helps us see something of the dilemma; she puts it like this: "I'm not sure how one is supposed to treat one's stepmother while one's own mother is alive. I don't know what the relationship is supposed to be." Dorothy went on to tell us that she got on very well with her stepmother and actually preferred her to her natural mother.

In addition to telling us what they felt about step-parents some referred to another aspect of remarriage, their fears that the second time around might also end in divorce. "That is something I could not tolerate," Vicky (fourteen) told us and certainly those who had experienced just this situation echoed Vicky's feelings. Lynn, her brother and sisters, experienced a second divorce. "It's so painful to see it happening all over again," she told us. And Larry, who was twelve when his mother remarried, found that four years later the marriage had broken up. "I felt it was most unfair to me," Larry told us. "I had made a positive investment and adjustment to this second marriage." The investment that Larry refers to was a common theme with those, few in number, who lived through a second divorce. They clearly felt cheated, angry, and resentful. They shared with others the view that a parent should consider the children's needs when choosing a second partner, not only their own, and they expected the parent, especially a father, to choose the right person for all of them.

## References

**1. 2.**   Opie, I. and Opie, P. (1980): *The Classic Fairy Tales*, London: Granada Publishing Limited.
**3.**   Central Statistical Office, Social Trends. (1980): Vol. 11. London: HMSO

## Notes

Research into step-relationships suggests that these can present problems and generate tension and anxiety. Maddox, 1975,[4] Robinson, (1980).[5] It has been found that children rate relationships with natural parents as being more important than those with step-parents. (Essen and Lambert, 1977).[6] Children do not want to have their natural parent replaced or displaced, unless there are very special reasons for this. The relationship has the best chance of succeeding when the step-family recognizes clearly that it is different from a natural family and the relationship between a step-parent and a child is different from the relationship the child has with the natural mother or father (Burgoine and Clarke, 1983).[7]

**4.**   Maddox, B. (1975): *The Half Parent*, London: André Deutsch. Reprinted (1980) as *Step-Parenting*. London: Unwin Paperbacks.
**5.**   Robinson, M. (1980) "Step Families: A Reconstituted Family System," *Journal of Family Therapy*, Vol. 2, No 1, 45–69, London: Academic Press.
**6.**   Essen, J. and Lambert, L. (1977): "Living in One Parent Families; Relationships and Attitudes of 16-Year Olds." *Child: Care, Health and Development*, 3, 301–318. London: National Children's Bureaux.

7.   Burgoine, J. and Clarke, D. (1983): Reconstituted Families in Rapoport R. N,
     Fogarty M. P. and Rapoport R, Eds. *Families in Britain*, London, for British
     Commission on Family Research. London: Routledge and Kegan Paul.

A conference to launch a National Step-Family Association was held in London in
April 1983.
Contact: The National Stepfamily Association, Mavis House, Mavis Lane,
Thrumpington, Cambridge CB2 2LB.

# CHAPTER 9

# FOUR PROFILES

Four distinct profiles emerged from our study of children's views and reactions to divorce: a child who has been harmed by divorce; a child who benefited by it; a child for whom the effect is mixed; and a child on whom divorce has had little or no effect. Each child had had a different set of experiences during and immediately following separation. It is this that counts and not what the family was like before divorce.

These profiles are not of individual children, but each represents a group of children. They are a collage made up of similar experiences and similar outcomes. They are based on subjective self-evaluation of how divorce has affected each child in the long run rather than immediately. This is how the divorce seemed to each participant and these were the long-term consequences from their point of view. Some of the lasting consequences were described as "good", others as "bad". If it was not clear to which category they were being ascribed we asked for clarification. For instance, was a cautious attitude to marriage considered an asset or a hindrance? Was the child pleased or sorry about growing up quickly and assuming responsibility at an early age? We also asked if a particular attitude was seen as relating directly to divorce and only included it if a connection was stated.

Those taking part in the study fell into one of the four profile groups and this is how they were distributed:

| | |
|---|---|
| Mixed profile (those for whom the consequences were mixed) | 32 |
| Negative profile (those for whom the consequences were all bad) | 26 |
| No effect profile (those on whom divorce has had little or no effect) | 25 |
| Positive profile (those on whom divorce has had a positive effect) | 17 |
| Total | 100 |

The consequences of divorce were described to us as a number of recurring themes in slightly different words. Similar consequences were described by all age groups, though older participants have had more time to reflect and develop insight. Where there are considerable differences between age groups, this is indicated.

These were some of the "bad" consequences:

| | |
|---|---|
| Feeling upset about poor communication | 43 |
| Difficulties in making long-term relationships | 34 |
| Feeling persistently sad | 29 |
| Bad effect on education | 24 |
| Feeling insecure | 25 |
| Lack of self-confidence | 17 |
| A decrease in the circle of relatives and other important people | 14 |
| Physical symptoms, depression, heavy drinking | 14 |

The consequences that were considered "good" were:

| | |
|---|---|
| Good understanding of people and relationships and ability to get on well with others | 45 |
| Becoming mature and responsible at an early age | 21 |
| Knowing a wider range of relatives and other important people | 20 |
| Good effect on education | 9 |

## Negative profile

By far the greatest number in this group shared with us their lasting feelings of unhappiness and resentment generated by poor communication about divorce. Many were still angry with one or both parents and in many cases a previously good relationship deteriorated or a poor one got worse because of the lack of proper explanation and sensitivity to the child's feelings at the time of separation. Those whose parents blamed each other were resentful and those who were grown-up and had children of their own did not want one grandparent to speak badly of the other in front of the grandchildren. Comments on communication are fully described in the chapter on communication.

Attitudes to marriage and relationships were significantly affected among young adults for whom they were a possibility or already in existence. This was not so with the younger age groups who did not show any strong feelings on the subject and no more of whom expressed doubts than those who hoped to get married one day.[1] A number of adults had a very cautious attitude, ranging to scepticism, which according to them was directly linked to their parents' poor relationship and marriage breakdown. Some of these adults were longing for a close and lasting relationship, but were afraid to risk involvement for fear that it would not last. They were afraid that they might have to go twice through the pain of losing someone they loved: once as a child and once as an adult. They found it hard to believe that anything could last. Some applied this only to themselves, others had a totally sceptical attitude to marriage generally and did not believe it could ever work for anyone.

Feelings of sadness and depression sometimes emerged at the time of separation and persisted for many years. This was not always so. Some did not remember feeling sad, or indeed feeling anything at first, but sadness was a response to finding out that a parent was lost for ever, for instance when the child or adult discovered that a parent they had not seen for some time was dead. In some cases it was only in adulthood or late adolescence that feelings of sadness could be safely acknowledged, when identification and dependence on the parent the child was living with was no longer total and when such feelings could be coped with or help was available from friends and others.

There was sadness about the lack of opportunity to get to know a parent, to find out what a parent was really like, instead of relying on the sometimes biased views of others. There was also guilt and sadness about condemning or rejecting a parent and not being able to make amends.

Very few wished that their unhappily married parents had stayed together – except the youngest children. Many felt sad about not having happily married parents and not knowing what a happy home atmosphere was like. Sadness was generated by having lost something the child had once had, or never having had what was considered "good" and the child's right. Feelings of sadness were for some so pervasive that they invaded every aspect of their lives and prevented full enjoyment of good things in the present.

Feelings of insecurity were carried by some children into their later years. Children who felt bewildered and insecure at the time of separation did not always recover and adopt a trusting attitude to life. The unforeseen always seemed to be round the corner and it was bad happenings that were anticipated rather than good.

Many adults who were satisfied with their present circumstances and had stable jobs and families traced their feelings of insecurity to how they remembered themselves as children at the time of separation: insecure and afraid of the future, not knowing what it would bring, how a single parent would manage, and who would look after him or her.

Insecurity was sometimes seen as being linked with lack of self-confidence. In some instances we were told that a child needed the encouragement and support of both parents to feel confident and acquire a sense of worth. This was specially true of children who did not get much encouragement from the parent they lived with, because the parent seemed worried or preoccupied. The other parent was out of the picture and there were no substitutes. These children felt they were not encouraged to do well at school and in various activities and were not praised for their achievements.

In some cases illness was thought to be related to divorce. A variety of persistent physical symptoms were described. These were connected with feeling unhappy, for instance missing a parent and being upset about the permanent loss. In a few cases persistent feelings of depression or heavy drinking were seen as resulting from a particularly unhappy situation continuing after divorce. A few of the adults and adolescents have had psychiatric treatment for depression and their condition medically diagnosed as such. A few more said they might have been clinically diagnosed as depressed if they had sought medical treatment, but they did not.

Not only did a great number of children lose touch with one parent, but also at the same time with others connected with the parent. This included grandparents, other relatives and friends. Many regretted this as yet another permanent loss resulting from divorce. They were no longer in touch with people they loved or liked and who were good to them and perhaps quite "special". Their circle had contracted.

Often living with a single parent meant a new circle of friends and loss of old friends through moving house if this was necessary. If the new circle of friends was compared unfavourably with the old, this was yet another 'negative' consequence of divorce.

The effect of divorce on education was considered negative by a considerable number. This happened in two ways: following the family upheaval some children did less well at school. They were worried, preoccupied, and not able to concentrate. They thought they might have done better in their examinations if they had been in a happier frame of mind.

Some children left school at the earliest possible opportunity, even though they would have preferred to continue their education in order to relieve their parent of the burden of supporting them or to help bring up younger siblings.[2] Of those who left school earlier than they wanted to some resumed their education many years later, as, for instance, did some married women with children. Others had to settle for jobs they would not have chosen and felt the chance of a good education and the career they had hoped for was lost.

Those with a negative profile shared some characteristics and have travelled a similar path since divorce. Adults were more highly represented than younger age groups. Their parents were divorced at a time when attitudes towards divorce were less permissive than today. A number of children grew up feeling at some stage different to other children.

Those whose parents divorced some years ago were often ashamed of having divorced parents. This was specially so if the family's religious beliefs condemned divorce or forbade it altogether. What other significant people such as neighbours, friends, and teachers thought was also important to the child. Some children believed it was shameful to apply for a divorce and said it was the parent they liked less who had wanted divorce and had taken the necessary steps. Children who felt ashamed thought they and their families were inferior to others and there was something wrong with them.

Feeling different and ashamed was also related to growing up in financial circumstances which had deteriorated as a result of divorce and were compared unfavourably with those of other people the child knew. Some children knew their housing was inferior, their clothes second-hand. They could not have the things other children had such as school outings and holidays. They did not like having "free" school dinners.

Being an only child or the eldest was linked with a negative profile. In some families there was an expectation that only or eldest children should assume adult roles and replace the absent parent as companions and confidantes. The expectation could come from the single parent, the child or both.

Children who felt responsible for parents found it a heavy burden. They did not always know how to help. They did not like having a social life and leaving a parent alone. Some found it exceedingly difficult to leave home when the time came. A number of adults still felt responsible, more than they wanted to, many years after leaving home.

A child negatively affected had a bad relationship with the parent they were living with and often also with the other parent. Many children felt unwanted, rejected, or a burden financially and emotionally to a single parent or one who remarried. Some parents were seen as difficult: over-anxious, suspicious, or depressed. Before divorce there was another parent who was the recipient of such behaviour – now the child was alone at the receiving end, with nothing to counterbalance the impact.

Some children got on badly with step-parents. They felt totally replaced or jealous of having a rival for a parent's time and affection. The same applied to boyfriends and girlfriends.

The great majority in this group expressed dissatisfaction with custody and access arrangements and a number went to live with the parent with whom they did not originally live, not necessarily considering this an improvement. This is described more fully in the chapter on access.

The three factors which emerged as being of paramount importance in leading to a negative profile were poor communication at the time of separation, not having a good relationship with at least the parent who was looking after the child following separation, and a high degree of dissatisfaction with custody and access arrangements.

## Positive profile

A number of children, adults and specially those in their teens, believed that in some ways they had benefited by divorce.

In this group the greatest number spoke of the positive way in which the experiences related to separation had influenced their attitude to people and relationships. They thought they had wider knowledge and better understanding of different people and situations and were more tolerant than children brought up in two-parent families. They had known their parents' unhappy marriage as well as other people's happy ones. They were aware that there are many different kinds of family. This enabled them to get on better with friends. Some adults spoke of their eagerness to get married and to create the happy family they did not have as children. The adults in this group who were married highly appreciated a happy home environment which they and their spouse were able to create.

A number of adolescents and adults mentioned with some pride and pleasure that when they compared themselves with children in two-parent families they believed they became mature and responsible adults at an earlier age. They had been given responsibility and allowed to make decisions concerning themselves when they are young, but did not feel burdened with this responsibility. They thought that they were subjected to fewer burdensome restrictions than they would have been by two parents and had a great deal of trust placed in them. Social networks expanded for some. Through parental remarriage they acquired step-parents and grandparents. A number of children got on so well with a step-parent that they did not know whom they liked better, the parent or the step-parent. For these children the family had enlarged rather than contracted. Some parents and step-parents complemented each other in terms of personality and interests and the child had a wider range of people to relate to. In some cases relatives who disapproved of the parent who left and were not in touch while the marriage lasted resumed contact. In some cases neighbours and friends were helpful.

Some parents joined clubs for divorced and separated people and made new friends. The children were pleased for them and in this way also made new friends and joined in activities specially organized for the children of club members. This also made them aware that there were many others in similar circumstances.

A small number reported a positive effect on their education. Before separation they were doing badly at school, were unable to concentrate, and were constantly worried about what was happening at home. Following separation these worries disappeared. The child was able to get on better at school and with homework. Some children who went to boarding-schools spoke very positively of the good education they received.

All those who felt they had benefited by divorce also travelled a similar path, which was very different to the one taken by badly affected children. Generally the child's pre-divorce family and experiences had little effect on outcome. When there had been many arguments, violence, and tension in the family and the child knew about this or remembered one or both parents suffering as a result, relief at the time of separation spelt a positive outcome.

In contrast to the badly affected children, those with a positive profile remembered that their parents told them as much as they wanted to know at the time of divorce. They were given adequate reasons for it and their future was discussed with them. The children were encouraged to ask questions and given a chance to express their feelings, even if these were anger or disappointment with the parents. They felt their parents were frank and honest.

After separation such children got on well with both parents or at least the parent they lived with. There were many ingredients, according to our informants, of such a good relationship. The parent could be relied on. Their actions were predictable. They were there and not likely to disappear. These parents did not expect their children to act as grown-ups and take the place of an absent spouse or grown-up friend. The parent was seen as coping with whatever worries they had and enlisting the help of other adults. The parents were seen as loving and enjoying having the child, rather than being burdened by the responsibilities of daily care and decisions. Their relationship with the ex-spouse was separate from the spouse's relationship with the child. However well or badly they got on or thought about the ex-wife or ex-husband, they did not try to influence the child or make access difficult.

Another important factor was the child's view of access arrangements. These were such that they suited the parents and the child. Neither was the child let down with unpredictable access arrangements, nor burdened with rigid and inflexible ones which interfered with the child's life and disregarded his or her wishes. Children in this group expressed a great deal of satisfaction with access.

## Mixed profile

This group, the largest one, includes young children, teenagers and adults. Those who presented a mixed profile looked back on divorce with various feelings. There were some gains and some losses for them. It is not surprising that this is such a large group. Human reactions are often mixed and human situations hardly ever simple.

Many in this group felt sad about the separation and missed one parent, but benefited by a more relaxed atmosphere at home and were better able to concentrate at school and when doing their homework. They may have regretted the lack of good communication at the time of separation, but as a result learned how important it was to talk about most things with members of their family. Whereas contact was lost with some important people in the child's environment, other contacts were made and new relatives acquired or old ones regained.

Those with a mixed profile tended to report many changes and fluctuations in their relationship with the parents and also with parents' partners. They may have not got on well when they were young but it was much worse in adolescence. Their acceptance and approval of a step-parent may have lessened or increased as they grew up and got to know them better. Some children who initially disapproved of remarriage were pleased later on that their parent had company and they no longer had to feel responsible for the parent. Even if they disliked the step-parent or were indifferent towards them they were pleased that they were there.

The satisfaction that the children felt about custody and access arrangements also seemed to fluctuate. Regular and frequent access might have been appreciated by a young child. This degree of access was resented by the young person if the parent continued to expect it in adolescence. Some growing-up girls were embarrassed while alone with their father and would have preferred to have someone else around. Such feelings are normal in adolescence. The access situation, which can be an artificial and strained, made such feelings harder to manage.

When compared with the positive and negative profiles what those with a mixed profile felt about communication, relationship with the custodial parent, and custody and access arrangements was somewhere in the middle. They neither felt the extreme dissatisfaction of those with a negative profile nor the high degree of satisfaction of those with a positive profile.

## No effect profile

Those who make up this group reported that divorce has had no effect, or a small one, on their lives. Children under twelve were highly represented. Unlike adults whose parents divorced before current legislation was introduced, they usually knew at least one divorced family or perhaps several. Although they did not expect divorce in their own family, once it happened knowing others in a similar position made their own acceptable.

For those with a 'no effect' profile life went on as before. The majority got on as before with the parent they lived with and either continued to see a great deal of the other parent whom they loved or did not have much contact with one to whom they were never very close anyway. Children who had a very distant relationship with their fathers did not miss them and were content with occasional treats and birthday cards. They went to the same school, had the same circle of friends and relatives and did not notice any big changes in the family's financial situation. Children in this group were satisfied with whatever they had been told about divorce and with custody and access arrangements.

Included in this group were a few adults for whom nothing much changed over the years. Their stories were very different from those of the contented children. Their earliest memories were unhappy ones. They were lonely and did not remember a loving relationship with either parent. At the time of separation they were even more unhappy, insecure, and bewildered.

They found little pleasure in growing up, learning, or work. As adults they continued to feel unhappy and did not see much hope for themselves in the future. Their relationships with adults continued to be unhappy as they had always been. It was not divorce that made them unhappy – they were already that before the divorce and there had been no improvement in their circumstances.

There were many factors which did not relate significantly to the child's profile. We found that how the child remembered itself and its family before divorce did not make much difference. At separation the family composition changed; so did significant relationships, in different directions. Some improved, some deteriorated; some became closer, others more distant.

Such factors as the social class of the family's chief wage-earner and the grown-up child's type of education was not important. Other factors were of some importance, such as changes in financial circumstances if the child was worse off and felt worried and inferior. The child's position in the family was another factor.

Not all children were affected and those who were, were not all affected in the same direction by the fact that they had divorced parents. Three factors we found to be of utmost significance and it was these which largely determined the child's profile. They were the quality of communication, relationship with the parent with whom the child lived, and satisfaction with the access arrangements. Their importance cannot be over-emphasized.

## Notes

1. No significant differences in attitudes to marriage were found between sixteen-year-olds in one- and two-parent families in a study by:
   Essen, J. and Lambert, L. (1977) "Living in One Parent Families: relationships and attitudes of sixteen-year-olds." *Child: Care, Health and Development* Vol. 3 No. 5, pp 301–308.
2. Children living in one-parent families tend to leave school earlier than those in two-parent families. This was reported by:
   Lambert, L. "Living in One Parent Families": School-leavers and Their Future. *Concern*, No. 29, National Children's Bureaux, Autumn, 1978.

# CHAPTER 10

# CONCLUSIONS

Separation can be seen both as a single event in the life of a family and its members and as part of a continuing process of family formation and reorganization. Separation is preceded by the gradual disruption of a marital relationship which once might have been happy or at least had high expectations attached to it. Separation disrupts an established pattern of relationships: domestic, working, and financial arrangements. It sets in motion a trail of events which include one spouse remaining a full-time and the other becoming a part-time parent and the possibility of remarriage for one or both parents with new step-relationships for children and adults.

The complexity of divorce-related experience is such that no statement made about the effects of divorce on children can be made with total certainty. Yet, in spite of this uncertainty, important decisions have to be made by all those involved in divorce concerning custody, access, post-divorce relationships, and remarriage.

From our own research and the evidence of many divorce-related studies important conclusions seem to be emerging. Separation has both short and long-term effects on children and the two outcomes seem to be somewhat different.

Separation itself is experienced as a crisis which can to a large extent be understood in terms of crisis theory put forward by Caplan (1961).[1] Children do not expect divorce in their own family even in our society in which the divorce rate is high. Parental separation is a situation which is different from any other the child may have experienced in the past and the child's limited repertoire of coping mechanisms may not be adequate to meet this new contingency. The feelings and reactions to the news of separation as described by our study of children and adults point to the traumatic impact of the event.

The reactions of children and adults have to be seen as interrelated. Separation disrupts the lives of all family members. The reactions of adults have been described and analysed in a number of studies beginning with the pioneering work of Goode (1956).[2] His footsteps were followed by other researchers: Marsden (1969),[3] George and Wilding (1974),[4] Weiss (1975),[5] Hart (1976),[6] Hetherington (1978),[7] and (1979).[8] and Wallerstein and Kelly (1980).[9] In all these studies the adults were affected in a number of ways.

Among the effects there was a high incidence of physical illness, heavy drinking, and heavy smoking. Many divorcees developed a poor self-concept and loss of confidence in sexual and parental roles. Anxiety, depression, and excessive worry about the present and future were common, as were feelings of failure and guilt. Many custodial parents were overwhelmed by domestic responsibilities especially when trying to combine these with outside employment. For many, financial worry was the main burden. Hetherington[10] found a degree of domestic disorganization during the year following separation which meant chaotic mealtime and bedtime routines.

Mothers were inconsistent in matters of discipline and more harsh towards boys than girls. Fathers tended to be over-indulgent. These effects, however, did not last longer than one or two years in most families. Many parents were worried about the effect on children, though a considerable number in the George and Wilding sample did not think that the children missed their mothers. There could be a subjective element in this interpretation of children's behaviour by parents.

Children have also been found to be negatively affected during the year or so immediately following separation. Wallerstein and Kelly[11] in a study based on sixty Californian families, found that pre-school children were most affected and tended to regress, became clinging, and excessively anxious about the possibility of losing both parents. Adolescents were least affected and those aged seven to ten were in between in terms of adjustment. Hetherington[12] and associates found that four-year-old children who had recently experienced divorce showed marked differences in their play and peer relationships when compared with children from intact families. Their play was less imaginative, they were less able to reverse their actions and got on less well with peers, being more aggressive, more shy, and less frequently chosen as playmates. Boys were more negatively affected than girls and the effects were longer-lasting.

Most studies under-emphasize the positive effect that separation can immediately have on children by providing relief from domestic tension and violence. Also the value of communication at the time of separation cannot be over-emphasized. As our own research shows, many children had mixed feelings and experienced relief. Good communication at the time of separation helped children cope with separation at the time it happened and served as an insurance policy against effects in the long run. Pain and anxiety associated with loss and change are an integral part of living and cannot be altogether avoided. They can, however, be mitigated, particularly by open communication within the family.

Long-term effects of separation need to be distinguished from short-term ones. In the past many studies concentrated on the effects of the absence of the father on boys and girls on the underlying assumption that certain characteristics are sex-linked and that this is desirable. Such characteristics as assertiveness, bravery, willingness to explore, and academic achievement were seen as typically masculine, whereas sensitivity, warmth, and passivity as typically feminine. Bee (1974)[13] having compared the findings of several studies on the effects of father absence concludes that boys and girls are affected somewhat differently. The effect is greater on boys than on girls, particularly if the father has been absent since before the son's fifth birthday. Boys score low on typically male characteristics and develop typically feminine cognitive skills such as verbalization, but score low on quantitative tasks. Girls, specially during adolescence, have difficulty in relating to men and boys, displaying excessive assertiveness or shyness.

In the past and also currently the roles of mothers have been assumed to be different and both sociological and psychological theories have been put forward to account for the difference. Sociologists led by Talcott Parsons (1956)[14] defined the role of mothers as expressive and of fathers as instrumental. Freud and many of his followers regarded the child's oral tie to the mother as of primary importance, with father appearing on the scene during the oedipal stage and his presence being necessary for the satisfactory resolution of the oedipus conflict terminating in identification with the same-sex parent. Bowlby (1969)[15] and associates have placed great emphasis on the development of attachment behaviour and the importance of social rather than feeding interaction. Bowlby originally assumed that for most children attachment is to the mother-figure, though for some children this can be the father or a sibling, and some children form multiple attachments.

More recently the values attached to sex-linked characteristics have been questioned, as have their biological determinants. Socialization is now seen by many as being of paramount importance in shaping sex-linked behaviour. Parke (1981)[16] sums up the current situation by suggesting that mothers and fathers are equally capable of caring for their infants and children and providing nurturing and stimulation. Infants are also capable of forming an equally strong attachment to the parent of either sex. What in effect happens is that mothers spend more time with children than fathers and from an early age their activities differ. Fathers tend to spend more time on play with children while mothers spend more time on nurturant activities such as feeding, bathing, changing nappies. Mothers spend more time with girls and fathers with boys. Boys receive more intellectual stimulation and encouragement while girls are encouraged to be more dependent and intellectually less exploratory and persistent than boys.

The conclusion of our study is that in the long run children's adjustment is significantly influenced by communication and the post-divorce, rather than pre-divorce, relationship with both parents. Our volunteers described the ingredients of a "good" relationship with the full-time parent in terms of feeling loved and not considered a burden. This included believing that the parent was coping well. They were happy for the parent to have a good social life or to remarry, provided the child was included and not neglected. They also did not want their part-time parent replaced. Whatever children felt about their part-time parent they wanted to be allowed to have their own feelings and not be used as vessels for the custodial parent's feelings.

Satisfaction was linked to the quality of the relationship with the part-time parent as well as access arrangements and there was a strong connection between the two. It is difficult to love or feel loved by a parent with whom contact is infrequent or non-existent. Frequent contact on the other hand makes it possible for parent and child to know each other, to give support and tangible proof of love (their presence rather than gifts). Children who adjusted best and were happiest were those whose access arrangements met their needs — in younger children for regularity, in older ones for flexibility. Even children who did not get on particularly well with a parent usually preferred to have some contact. However, a small group of children who did not want access at all cannot be ignored. They were happy living with one parent, with little or no contact with the other. Such apparent indifference to the part-time parent appeared to be related to the non-existence of a bond before divorce. Some children remember very little interaction with their fathers and did not seem to know much about them. Resentment or idealization of an absent or unknown parent seemed to be associated with feeling abandoned or believing that contact was prevented or resented by the custodial parent. The custodial parent as well as the part-time one played a vital role in satisfaction with access. It was children who knew that both parents wanted and approved of access who remembered enjoying their meetings with the absent parent best.

Financial circumstances also played a part in post-divorce adjustment. Children who saw themselves as being adversely affected financially were both objectively and subjectively deprived. They were deprived of certain kinds of food, treats, holidays, decent housing. They were also deprived of a feeling of equality with their peers in comparison with whom they were poor and this resulted in a devalued self-image: not feeling as good as and different from others. Some children left school early for financial reasons.

The results of different studies are not strictly comparable, because of differences in samples, method of gathering data, and information sought. Allowing for this lack of strict comparability, our findings add weight to the findings of other recent studies, which are that children need not be harmed by divorce provided that they are brought into the discussions about separation, they are not materially deprived, continue to have a good relationship with both parents and are satisfied with the access arrangements. Ferri (1976),[17] whose findings were based on a sample of children taking part in a longitudinal study known as the National Child Development Study, came to the conclusion that behaviour previously attributed to children from broken homes could be accounted for by the material disadvantages. Inadequate income and poor housing were directly associated with poor school performance and early school-leaving.

Wallerstein and Kelly (1980)[18] found that the happiest and best adjusted children were those who had frequent, regular, and flexible contact with the non-custodial parent and could exercise some degree of control over visiting arrangements by being able to use their bicycles to circulate between the homes of their parents. It was the continuity of relationship with both parents that was of the utmost importance in helping children to cope with divorce and recover from its initial impact.

Another study, by Hess and Camara (1979),[19] compared three groups of children of divorced parents. Group A had a good relationship with both parents, Group B with one parent only, and Group C with neither parent. Children in Group A had lowest scores on stress and aggression and highest on work effectiveness and peer interaction. Group C was at the opposite end of the continuum. Group B had scores on stress and aggression only slightly higher than Group A. Thus children with a good relationship with both parents seemed to be best adjusted and those who had a good relationship with one parent were relatively unharmed. Those who did not get on well with either parent fared badly.

Rowlands (1981),[20] on the basis of contacts with many divorced parents also found that good access arrangements and a good relationship with the part-time parent which had the blessing of the custodial parent led to the happiest outcome. It seems that the importance to children of continuity of relationships with both parents cannot be over-emphasized. Sudden disruption of a significant bond, particularly when the loss cannot be talked about and mourned, sets in train reactions to separation which have been described by Bowlby. They include anger and sorrow. Such feelings may not be acknowledged as an immediate response and emerge many years after separation. Where no strong bond exists separation seems to cause little disruption.

The theoretical assumptions which guided us throughout and were previously described, helped us to understand how stages of development affected emotional responses to stress, such as the belief of younger children that their wishes would come true. We were also not surprised to find that intellectual functioning dictated the extent to which, at a particular age, a child was able to see things from not only his own but also the others' point of view. This was illustrated by the ability of adolescents and adults to describe their parents as a married couple. Attachment theory guided our understanding of immediate and delayed grief as a response to separation. Systems theory, with its emphasis on the importance of good communication and relationships between family members, directed our attention towards communication at the time of separation and the need to understand children's reactions in the context of other relationships within the family, such as the post-divorce arrangements between the parents and the parents' relationships with other systems outside the family such as relatives, neighbours, and school.

Our findings lend weight to the view that a child's future is not determined at any stage, but that harmful and potentially harmful experiences do not have a lasting influence if subsequently compensated for by good experiences. This inspires us with hope. It means that children can be helped to cope with the disruption caused by separation.

## Notes

1. Caplan, G. (1961): An Approach to Community Mental Health, London, Tavistock Publications.
   Caplan described crisis as a new situation such as illness, the birth of a baby or

any other which creates a psychic state of disequilibrium in which previously employed coping mechanisms are no longer adequate. A crisis is time-limited and lasts four to six weeks. At the end of this time a new equilibrium is reached which may be at a more or less mature level of functioning. Among other factors, the help available determines how a state of crisis is resolved and a little help at the right time can produce the maximum desirable change.

2.  Goode, Wm. (1965): *After Divorce*. New York: Free Press. Reprinted (1965) as WOMEN IN DIVORCE.
3.  Marsden, D. (1969): *Mothers Alone*. London: Allen Lane.
4.  George, and Wilding, P. (1972): *Motherless Families*. London: Routledge and Kegan Paul.
5.  Weiss, R. (1975): *Marital Separation*. New York: Basic Books.
6.  Hart, N. (1976): *When Marriage Ends*. London: Tavistock Publications.
7.  Hetherington, M. et al, *The Aftermath of Divorce* in Stevens, J. H. and Mathews, M. (1978): eds. *Mother-Child, Father-Child Relations*. Washington D. C. National Association for the Education of Young Children.
8.  Hetherington, M. et al, 'Play and Social Interaction in Children Following Divorce.' (1979): *Journal of Social Issues*, 35, 26–49.
9.  Wallerstein, J. and Kelly, J. B. (1980): *Surviving the Breakup*. London: Grant McIntyre.
10. Hetherington (5) op.cit.
11. Wallerstein and Kelly, op. cit.
12. Hetherington, M. (8) op. cit.
13. Bee, H. (1974): "On the importance of Fathers." *Social Issues in Developmental Psychology*. London: Harper and Row.
14. Parsons, Talcott, and Bales, R. F. (1956): *Family: Socialisation and Interaction Process*, London: Routledge and Kegan Paul.
15. Bowlby, J. (1969): *Attachment*. London: The Hogarth Press.
16. Parke, J. (1981): *Fathering*. London: Fontana.
17. Ferri, E. (1976): *Living in a One Parent Family*. London: NFER Publishing Company.
18. Wallerstein and Kelly, op. cit.
19. Hess, R. D. and Camara, D. A., "Post-Divorce Relationships as Mediating Factors in the Consequences of Divorce for Children." *Journal of Social Issues*, 35, 79–96.

# CHAPTER 11

# WHO CAN HELP AND HOW

The suggestions put forward in this chapter are addressed to individuals, groups or social systems which directly or indirectly affect the child of divorced parents. They are made on the assumption that no child can be understood and helped in isolation. A child is a member of his or her natural or substitute family. The relationships between family members, and the family's contacts with the systems outside its own boundaries: relatives, neighbours, professional helpers, schools, the law, employment and welfare provisions, all have a direct bearing on the development and wellbeing of each individual child.[1] Our opening remarks are addressed to those most directly involved in the process of divorce. The circle then is enlarged to include other groups and systems. We conclude with a view on parenting outside marriage.

## Parents

To a young child, the most important people in the world are its parents. It is they who provide for the child's physical, emotional and social needs. Through early contacts the child gains a sense of trust and becomes social. As the child grows up the relationship changes. The role of parents does not diminish in importance, it becomes different. It is therefore parents who are the first line of defence against the immediate impact of divorce. At this stage it is parents who can best provide explanations suited to the child's age, personality and circumstances. A distressed child or young person may find it hard to take in explanations and parents need to be sensitive to this. Children's wishes need to be taken into account when considering the future. It is a good assumption that no child is ever too young to be spoken to even if it cannot grasp all that is said. Parents talk to their babies about all kinds of things long before the baby is able to reply.

Children need to be encouraged to ask questions and reveal their fears. They need permission to express feelings which they are afraid may hurt their parents. At a time when parents may have very negative feelings towards each other, they must assure the child that he or she is not expected to take sides. The child has every right to contact with both parents even if they do not want to have contact with each other. Parents cannot be dishonest about their feelings towards each other. It is more important to clarify what these feelings are, to whom they belong, and at whom they are directed.

## Children

Older children particularly, but younger ones also can help their parents by understanding how upset they may feel. Children can help too by making their wishes clear on matters of custody and access, without guilt or the fear of hurting parents. It is the parents who have decided to separate – it is their decision. Faced with this fact, children should exercise their right to choice and to having two parents.

## Relatives, friends and neighbours

It is to their informal networks that most families turn for assistance before they even consider professional help. A child can derive great comfort from knowing that their parent is not isolated. The period of transition from being a two-parent to a single-parent family can be particularly difficult. Making sure the family is not alone on special occasions such as Christmas can be very important. Practical help by relatives or friends such as baby-sitting and occasionally having the children to stay enables the single parent to create a new social life and relieve the tension which family closeness often brings. Single parents often have difficulty in distinguishing between the normal ups and downs which accompany developmental stages and the unhappiness and problems related to separation. Relatives and friends, specially those who themselves have children, can often reassure an anxious single parent that their children behave in exactly the same way. The part-time parent may welcome sharing activities and outings with another family.

Relatives and friends who are closer to one ex-spouse than the other often take sides. This attitude is very common and many divorcees find comfort in being told that their marriage is best ended. Those who are told that "they should have tried harder" find the disapproval of others distressing. If sides are taken by relatives and friends then "not in front of the children" is a good rule. Most children love both parents and need to think of them as real people with good and bad characteristics. Growing up believing that one parent is totally bad does not bode well for the child's future. He or she may be afraid of taking after the "bad" parent and to feel rejected and abandoned by mother or father is painful. To love such a parent is difficult, if not impossible.

## Teachers

Apart from parents or those who act as parents, the most influential adults in a child's life are teachers. "For almost a dozen years during a formative period of their development children spend almost as much of their waking life at school as at home. Altogether this works out at some 15000 hours (from the age of five until school-leaving) during which schools and teachers may have an impact on the development of the children in their care." (Rutter 1971)[2] On the basis of a major study based on twelve secondary shools in London, Rutter comes to the conclusion that pupils' behaviour and attainment are strongly influenced by the general ethos of the school and the way each child is treated as an individual. On reviewing some fifty studies, Rosenshine (1971)[3] found that the two most important teacher characteristics influencing pupils' achievement were warmth and enthusiasm. Children who fail to learn and do not achieve their full potential do so for a variety of reasons. Emotional obstacles feature prominently among them and teachers are in a good position to understand and help to remove these obstacles. There is no doubt that teachers are extremely important in a child's life. The expectations of a teacher have been found to play a particularly significant part in achievement. A child who is expected to do well is more likely to do so than a child who is expected to fail.

Because of the high proportion of single-parent families in the population and a high concentration in some areas such as the inner London boroughs any infant, junior, or secondary school teacher is likely to have in his or her class a number of children who are at various stages of parental divorce. Some of these children may be living in fear, hope, or both that their parents' marriage will break up. They may feel that their place is at home rather than at school, so that they can keep the parents together, intervene in parental fights and generally keep abreast of what is happening. Anxiety may keep the child at home or make him or her inattentive during lessons. Anxiety may also lead to aggression or prevent the child making friends at school.

There may also be children whose parents very recently separated and the child is experiencing the full impact of a domestic crisis. They may be fully involved in parental recriminations about the broken marriage and arguments about property, money, access and having to cope with divided loyalties. At this stage children are usually very insecure and fearful about the future. There may also be a strong feeling of relief from tension and the child may be glad that the parents are no longer together. Immediately following separation the child's school performance may deteriorate, but this decline need not be permanent. Once the child has settled into a new routine and begun to accept the new shape of his or her family with a stable access arrangement, school performance may dramatically improve and relationships with teachers and peers may become more trusting and friendly.

For many children separation brings new roles and responsibilities. Girls who live with their fathers may be expected to take on the household chores, leaving less time for homework. Children may be late for school because they did not have enough sleep or the parent who was responsible for waking them up and getting them off is no longer there. The parent with whom the child lives may be trying to rebuild his or her social life and leave the child alone in the evening. Parents often do not realize that even older children are afraid to be alone in the house, and older children do not like to admit to such fears. The result is that the child is afraid to fall asleep and so has difficulty in getting up.

Children show their distress and unhappiness in many different ways. Younger children may cry and reveal obvious unhappiness. Older ones may try to cover up distress only to show it through their school work. Some children may wish to leave school for financial reasons.

Although certain teachers are assigned special pastoral responsibilities for their pupils' welfare, all teachers will increasingly have contact with children affected by divorce, and there are a number of ways in which they can help. Younger children may need physical comforting. Simple actions like giving a child a hug may go a long way. All children appreciate being given the chance to share their fears and worries. Even if they do not take advantage of the offer, they find it is good to know that the opportunity is there. All that an older child may need is the knowledge that the teacher is aware of the child's home circumstances and their impact. Not intentionally, but through lack of thought, it can be easy for a teacher to embarrass a child in front of his school-mates by asking questions about his family circumstances. Such matters are private.

Hopefully the days when children from "broken homes" were expected to do badly in every aspect of their development will soon be over. Much damage can be done to a child as a result of such expectations. Teachers can help by accepting the "normality" of each child's family while recognizing pain and distress. Whereas this can cause temporary setbacks in a child's progress, it need not be permanent if the right kind of help is available at the right time. Few people are in a better position to offer it than a teacher because children and teachers share the same space – the school – for a sizeable part of the day.

Teachers also have contacts with the child's family. The nature of these depends on the willingness of parents and teachers to create a partnership. The difficulties which a child is experiencing at home may have direct bearing on the child's progress at school and the choices made about leaving school and a future career. A good partnership between teachers and parents can help the child. Teachers may become involved in the arrangements which parents make for contact with the school and for receiving school reports; both parents may wish to be involved in this.

## Doctors

When adults distressed by the breakup of their marriage seek professional help, they initially tend to go to their doctor.[4,5] It is the general practitioner who knows the family and who can deal with many physical symptoms caused by distress. Younger children may regress to earlier modes of behaviour such as enuresis, encopresis, excessive clinging to the parent they live with, and fearfulness. Older children complain of tummy-aches, headaches, and nightmares, or wish to stay away from school.

Doctors are in a unique position to help because of their knowledge of the family circumstances and being regarded as safe recipients of confidential information. If the symptoms they are presented with are related to distress they understand this and can draw attention to the child's unhappiness. Unhappy parents are not always able to see clearly and face their child's distress. A general practitioner may be either able to help the family directly or refer them to specialized services such as Child Guidance clinics which are community-based and Departments of Family and Child Psychiatry which are usually hospital-based. Both can offer the services of a psychiatric team, which consists of all or some of the following: a child psychiatrist, psychotherapist, clinical psychologist, remedial teacher, and social worker. The contributions of these disciplines are described in the literature on child psychiatry and family therapy (Lask, J. and Lask, B. (1981)).[6]

Some family therapists have developed special interest and techniques in working with divorced families with a view to preserving the continuity of post-divorce parenting while drawing suitable boundaries and rules for the new post-divorce family unit (Black, D. (1982),[7] Bentovim, A. and Gilmour, L. (1981)).[8]

## Social workers

Social workers are employed by statutory agencies such as local authorities and voluntary organizations such as Family Service Units. The majority are based in social services area teams, others in day care and residential settings. A small number are based in hospitals, general practices, schools, and psychiatric services. Education Welfare Officers are employed by local education authorities. Probation Officers and Court Welfare Officers are attached to the courts. Some voluntary agencies, such as the National Marriage Guidance Council, work through carefully selected and highly trained volunteers.

In whatever setting social workers find themselves they come into contact with a large number of families with divorce problems. These may range from ignorance about welfare rights to feelings of loss and depression in both children and adults and the inability to reorganize family life effectively following separation. In some cases problems may be presented explicitly. Sometimes a request for one kind of help may be an indirect request for another; for example, a request for a day nursery place may be based on a single mother's wish to work. It may also be a result of not being able to cope with a child who, following separation, has been difficult to manage, having regressed at a time when the mother herself feels depressed, depleted of self-confidence, and finding it hard to manage financially. A high proportion of children in residential care are from one-parent families.

There are many different ways in which social workers can help. Separation is a crisis in the life of all family members. Even when preceded by a long period of expectation and preparation, the event itself is never totally anticipated and the individual's and family's previous coping mechanisms may prove inadequate. Help, to be effective, needs to be given speedily, and a professional helper's long waiting list may mean it comes too late, when a little at the right time might have gone a long way (Caplan (1961)).[9]

Separation is often accompanied by a breakdown in communication. By getting the family together and enabling all members, including young children, to talk to each other, a social worker fulfils a very useful role. Very often all that is needed is a letter of invitation, a room, and enough chairs for everyone to sit down. The social worker acts as an enabler and, while recognizing that the marriage has broken down, symbolizes the continuity of parental roles.

Distressed and angry ex-spouses find it very hard to talk to their children about what is happening and to refer to each other without recrimination. A social worker may tactfully point out that the task is not to exchange mutual accusations, but to talk about future arrangements.

Many adults and particularly children may feel bewildered and think they have no control over their situation. They may need a simple explanation of the meaning of such terms as custody, access, care and control. Few people are fully aware what choices are open to them and are baffled by the legal process. There are many practical matters to be resolved when a couple separate relating to property, maintenance, and claiming benefits. The welfare rights entitlement is a maze, understood by very few members of the public and only the select few who are highly trained welfare rights experts. If the social worker does not possess enough expertise, she or he should ensure that it is available to the client from a Legal Advice Centre, a solicitor or such organizations as One-Parent Families or Child Poverty Action Group. These organizations publish useful pamphlets and information sheets.

Human needs are diverse and both practical and emotional. Loss of a spouse and partial loss of a parent through separation arouses many feelings which are similar to those encountered in bereavement. The lost person needs to be given up, a new identity found and a life created in a world which no longer contains the lost person. A "bereaved" parent may have a diminished capacity to parent, less energy and less responsiveness to the needs of children. Children can be helped indirectly by the parent's restored ability to manage and regained confidence. Many single parents doubt their capacity to be a good parent outside a couple relationship. They need help to gain confidence and assurance about the normality of their situation.

Direct help can also be offered to children, to enable them to understand what has happened. Younger children particularly may need assurance that they are not so omnipotent as to have caused the breakup of the parents' marriage and that their mother and father still love the child even if they are not able to look after the child who is in residential care. For some children it is hard to be loyal to both parents and not to take sides. They must be assured of their right to remain neutral. Children who feel responsible for their parent need to hear that parents are not their responsibility – it is the other way round. Whatever feelings are experienced – sadness, anger, relief – they need to be shared and acknowledged as valid and appropriate to the situation. Knowing that there are many other children in the same boat may not relieve sadness, but will at least help the child know that she or he is not a freak and "different".

Many non-custodial parents, even if access is given willingly, find access periods quite daunting. They find it hard just to be together with their child and consider the circumstances abnormal. This results in a frantic search for some special gift each time the child is seen, or some special activity. Practical advice from a social worker may be appreciated and Peter Rowlands' book *Saturday Parent* is a mine of information and sound practical advice on what to do and pitfalls to avoid.[10]

Social workers who are school-based or attached to courts are in a particularly favourable position to offer help to divorcing families. Those who are based in other agencies should make their services known by advertising them widely and perhaps have a special time when divorcing parents can drop in informally, without feeling that they have a major problem needing drastic remedy. Many working parents are only able to come after working hours or on Saturday and this needs to be taken into account.

## Health Visitors

On average a divorcing couple with children would have been married about ten years. The children therefore, are young. For this reason, because of their routine contact with young families, health visitors are likely to be visiting a large number of divorced families.

Health visitors are seen by the public as health educators, concerned with prevention of illness and promotion of good health in the widest sense. A health visitor is in a unique position as she visits all families, not just those who are in trouble. This often makes her more easily acceptable to the family than, say, a social worker. A health visitor may be the first person to realize that a child is not thriving and she will be aware of possible reasons for this: the child may not understand the meaning of events which have taken place, may not understand why one of the parents has left home, and may be pining for his or her presence and company.

Young children are particularly vulnerable at the time of separation. They do not understand what is happening without repeated, simple explanations. The adults in the family often do not talk to young children, assuming that they would not understand, that they will not miss an absent parent and forget him or her very quickly. Whereas the custodial parent may be willing to grant access to older children, they may be more reluctant to do so with a young child for several reasons: sometimes the father is considered not able to look after the young child properly during access periods; should the custodial parent remarry, the child may think that a step-parent is the real parent. Young children who grow apart from their real parents develop fantasies about them and may imagine an idealized figure as someone totally bad who abandoned them. If the real reason for separation is not understood, the young child is likely to imagine that it is all his or her own fault.

A health visitor may be able to help a parent understand better what the child is feeling and thinking, talk to the child directly or, in some circumstances, refer to a social worker or other specialized agency.

## The legal system

The courts have been concerned with the judiciary as well as welfare aspects of laws relating to children in divorce since 1857. Since then various Acts of Parliament have included provisions for the children of the family.[11] Although the principle that the welfare of the child should be of paramount importance has repeatedly been stated in successive Acts relating to divorce, what constitutes "the welfare of the child" has not been defined. Court decisions are often made in accordance with unwritten rules governed to a large extent by principle, attitude, and precedent.

An overview of court decisions in custody cases by M. Richards (1981)[12] reveals four principles: firstly, the courts are reluctant to disturb the status quo. Thus the arrangements made immediately following separation are likely to be approved by the court and continue. These may not be necessarily the best long-term arrangements. They might have been made hastily and treated by one or both parties as temporary. Thus the status quo is not necessarily in the child's best interest.

Secondly, other things being equal, mothers are presumed more capable of bringing up a child alone than fathers. This appears to be a continuation of sex-segregated roles within marriage. In 80 percent of cases it is the mother who is granted custody. Fathers are often discouraged from seeking custody by their solicitors or do not apply because they see little chance of winning. They are also influenced by social attitudes and expectations and consider that bringing up children is a woman's job. Thus inequality begins within marriage and continues following separation.

Thirdly, the courts do not favour joint custody orders on the assumption that they may only lead to further trouble and enable marital strife to continue after divorce. Within marriage both parents have the custody of their children; when marriage ends the presumption is that only one parent can continue to be a proper parent.

Fourthly, access is regarded as unimportant. Access orders are not made in one-third to one-half of divorce cases. The courts may assume that reasonable arrangements will be made between parents. This does not always work out in practice, and many children lose touch with one parent.

The present system is adversarial. Each party has his or her own solicitor, while the child is not represented. The role of the existing courts is traditionally viewed by the public in terms of apportioning blame, penalizing the wrongdoer, and of adjudication between contestants. This image persists when family matters are brought before the courts and the atmosphere is not conducive to emphasis on the welfare of children and amicable settlements between parents.

There is a need for a fundamental change in the law, its administration, and underlying assumptions and attitudes. The Finer Report[13] recommended the introduction of Family Courts, retaining their judicial function, but with emphasis on family welfare and making services readily available as an integral part of the process of divorce. The introduction of such courts, dealing with all family matters except cases falling within criminal law, would bring many advantages. The dual system of law would cease to exist with the abolition of the matrimonial jurisdiction of Magistrates' Courts. The atmosphere would be more conducive to amicable settlement of all matters regarding children and finance. All those administering family law would have special expertise and the benefit of knowledge and accumulated experience. In time, the public would come to view the Family Courts as a judicial institution concerned with welfare rather than crime and punishment.

Although the law cannot legislate for attitudes it can influence them, particularly by radically changing attitudes and legislation relating to custody. The best interest of the child would be served by making decisions after careful consideration of all the circumstances, taking the wishes of the parents and the children into consideration. Regardless of the parent's sex, his or her ability to provide for the child's physical, emotional, social, and educational needs would be considered. Another factor to be taken into consideration would be mutual willingness to encourage contact between both of the parents and the child. By making joint custody orders the rule and depriving one parent of custody an exception, the law would give the right kind of message to parents and encourage, rather than discourage, as it does at present, sensible behaviour. Only the principle of joint custody can emphasize the continuity of parenting and the child's right to have two parents.

There are, of course, exceptional circumstances such as mental or physical cruelty, deliberate abandonment of the child or refusal to maintain when the parent is able to do so. These should be the sole grounds for depriving a parent of custodial rights and obligations.

Since care and control can effectively be only given to one parent, the courts need to place much more emphasis on access and if necessary to define it much more strictly than they are now inclined to do.

At present the involvement of Court Welfare Officers is minimal. There should be far greater involvement of an independent person, ideally in every case where children are concerned, to report on the circumstances, assure the court that appropriate arrangements have been made, to make recommendations when the arrangements made by parents do not seem to be in the child's interest, and last, but not least, to offer conciliation service to the whole family. The post could be filled by a qualified social worker with experience of family work, employed by either Social Services Departments or the Probation and After Care Service.

The idea of conciliation is not entirely new. Social workers, including probation officers and marriage guidance counsellors, have for many years provided a counselling service to divorcing families. What is new is a more formal recognition of conciliation and the appearance of specialized pioneering agencies such as The Bristol Courts Family Conciliation Service[14] and the Family Court Unit of the Leicestershire Probation Service.[15] The Finer Report[16] defined conciliation as "assisting the parties to deal with the established breakdown of their marriage by reaching agreements, or giving consents or reducing the area of conflict upon custody, support, access, and education of children". Currently an interdepartmental government committee is considering the scope and future of conciliation. With a rising divorce rate, the idea of conciliation advice needs urgent implementation. The service should be provided by professionals, available to all divorcing parents, easily accessible, without stigma and fully family-orientated, so that all members are involved in coming to terms with the past, understanding their current situation, and making the best possible plans for the future.

## Social Policy

It is often said that this country has no consistent or recognizable social policy relating to the family and this includes single-parent families. The state often takes away with one hand what it has given with the other. At the present time the role of the state in welfare provision is controversial: some people advocate more, others less, public spending, depending on their political affiliation. The role of the family is also controversial. Some wish the family to bear the main burden of supporting its dependants, others argue for more state support. Whether mothers of young children should work and entrust the care of under-fives to others is another debated issue. There is no evidence that children are harmed by having a working mother and some evidence that, provided suitable arrangements are made for the child, the child's wellbeing is enhanced by the mother's satisfaction with her various roles, including mothering and work.

There are three areas particularly in which social policy affects divorced single-parent families: employment, day care provision, and family income maintenance.

There has been in recent years a trend towards greater participation in the labour force by all women, including mothers with dependent children, though mothers of under-fives are less likely to be working, or working full-time, than mothers of children over five. In 1980 (Great Britain) 17 percent of mothers with dependent children worked full-time and 36 percent part-time. (Source CMS 1980 tables 5.3 and 5.4 OPCS 1982). Single mothers and fathers may choose to work for many reasons. They may enjoy the company of others at work, feel that work enhances social status, and for financial reasons. Few single mothers are able to live on maintenance and the Law Commission[17] has recently suggested that maintenance between ex-spouses should be a temporary measure to facilitate transition from married to single status. To meet the needs of single parents employment opportunities should include refresher courses for those who have been out of the labour field for some time, flexible working hours, opportunities for part-time work and long holidays which coincide with children's school holidays.

If a single parent is to have a real choice between working and staying at home, there is great need for adequate day care facilities. Family centres with emphasis on a family-oriented approach and a stimulating environment have replaced many of the old-fashioned day nurseries with their emphasis on physical care. There are far too few such day centres and many more are necessary. There is also need for an expansion in the provision of daily child minders, who are registered as suitable by local authorities. The Study Commission on the Family (1983)[18] came to the conclusion that "...despite wide recognition of their value, pre-school facilities are still far from adequate". A great expansion is needed including day centres for school-age children, who need to be cared for during school holidays.

A series of proposals has been put forward by various bodies to alleviate poverty experienced by one-parent families. These families are one of the poorest sections of society. Compared with two-parent families, their income is lower and a much higher proportion are on social security for long periods, thus living at subsistence level. Some do not claim social security and live on low earnings and maintenance below the subsistence level defined by social security. The financial disadvantage which follows separation stems from long-standing social attitudes to marriage break-down, the reluctance to condone divorce and fear that if one-parent families fare reasonably well the demise of the family might be brought about. The Beveridge proposals which laid the foundations of the welfare state embodied the principle that women were male dependants while all family members were treated as parts of families rather than as individual units. The principle of insurance was not extended to cover divorce. Thus a situation was created in which divorced women have not been able to claim against their own or their ex-husband's insurance. Maintenance payments have been low and the major resource has been supplementary benefit, not originally designed to cater for large sections of the population, but only for those ineligible for contributory benefits.

The Finer Report[10] proposed a guaranteed maintenance allowance. It recommended that this allowance should be independent of insurance contributions and financed by the government. This was to replace maintenance payments, be large enough to offer a genuine choice between working and staying at home, supplement low or part-time earnings, be available to all one-parent families, be easy to claim, and provide equity with but not advantage over two-parent families. Separate allowances were to be made for the parent and for the child. The parent's benefit would be tapered off according to earnings and stopped when earnings reached the level of average male earnings. Payment would also stop on cohabitation.

These proposals have not been implemented and as the number of single-parent families has grown considerably, their implementation would be even more timely now than when they were put forward in 1974. The disadvantage of the scheme is that it is means-tested and one of the causes of poverty is low take-up of means-tested benefits as proved by the low take-up of Family Income Supplement.

A more fundamental change would require everyone to be treated as a unit, rather than a member of a family. Under this scheme those looking after children would be credited with contributions and could then claim an allowance if they chose to stay at home or work part-time following divorce. The allowance would not be means-tested and claiming it would involve no stigma. Such a scheme would be based on a final acceptance of equity between the sexes in the welfare state.

There is now a considerable body of evidence linking poor school performance and leaving school at the earliest opportunity, with financial disadvantage.[19] In the past such consequences were thought to be associated with "broken homes". If financial measures to alleviate poverty are not introduced an ever-increasing number of children in divorced families will spend their formative years in poverty which will affect their health, school performance, and self-image.

## The Media

Films, television, and newspapers play a vital role in shaping attitudes to family life and divorce. The "typical" family portrayed on television following the Chancellor's budget speech, showing the effects of various measures on "an average family" usually consist of a working father, a housewife mother and two children. As the Study Commission on the Family[21] points out this is no longer either a typical or an average family. All that such a portrayal does is to devalue the self-image of any family and child who does not conform to this mythical standard. By portraying the divorcing family as "normal", while at the same time dealing openly with the consequences of divorce, the media could play a helpful role. Films about divorced families, such as *Kramer* v. *Kramer* and *Table for Five* have brought to public notice both the normality of divorce and some of the problems involved. Documentary films and television programmes could further disseminate knowledge about and shape attitudes to post-divorcing parenting.

## Parenting after divorce

Following divorce one parent becomes a full-time and the other a part-time parent. The roles of wife and mother and of husband and father are no longer linked and carried out by the same person. If one in five children born today is likely to have divorced parents by his or her sixteenth birthday, it is post-divorce parenting that now needs to be as widely recognized and receive as much attention as parenting within marriage. Perhaps we need to start applying some of the knowledge we already have about parenting to this new state of affairs. Writing some years ago about *The Child, the Family and the Outside World*, Winnicott (1968)[22] suggested that good mothering cannot be measured by the amount of time mother and child spend together, but is related to the satisfaction and enjoyment obtained from each other's company. Studies comparing children of working mothers with those of non-working mothers suggest that children of working mothers are not adversely affected by spending less time with the mother. These findings could be applied to part-time parenting. A part-time parent can be a good parent, positively influencing the child's development.

If mothers and fathers are equally capable of providing good parenting "Mother need not be a woman" (Schaffer, 1977)[23] then both parents should be free to choose between full-time and part-time parenting, without the guilt and remorse experienced particularly by mothers when they become part-time parents. Such a choice should be based on the parents' capabilities and preferences, the strength of the child's attachment bond to each parent, the child's own wishes, and practical considerations such as housing, employment, and availability of day care.

The roles of full-time and part-time parents differ. It is the full-time parent who cares for the child's daily needs ensuring that the child is well fed, properly clothed, has playmates and playthings, and someone immediately available to deal with emotional and physical hurt or illness. The full-time parent needs to provide guidance and discipline, ensure that rules are clear and the child does not hurt itself or anyone else. The school-aged child has to attend school and needs reasonable conditions for doing homework. Many single parents bring up their children very successfully when the part-time parent cannot be available. There can also be many substitutes within the kinship and friendship networks.

If the part-time parent can be available, the child and also the full-time parent will benefit in a variety of ways. The child can have two parental models instead of one. Because each parent is a different person, between them they have a wider range of characteristics, skills, and values, which the child can observe, learn, and choose from. Mother and father are biologically different. Having a good relationship with both enables a boy or girl to accept and value biological differences and to have the experience of being valued, loved and admired by two people of different sex. A sense of being valued is important for the child's self-image and is enhanced by being inspired by those people who are considered to be important by the child.

Many children living with a single parent tend to worry about the parent and what will happen if he or she becomes ill. Knowing that a part-time parent is available may lessen this anxiety.

Close relationships can become a source of tension. If a child can have another relationship outside the home, the atmosphere at home can be much happier. Looking after children is an emotionally demanding task and most parents welcome time away from their children. The part-time parent can relieve the full-time one of having continuous responsibility, by acting as a baby-sitter and having the child at weekends and during holidays.

Bringing up a family means financial responsibility. A part-time parent who has regular contact with the child may be more inclined to provide for the child financially, according to means. If giving the child special treats is based on recognition that this is something they can do, whereas there are many daily tasks which they cannot engage in, these treats are less likely to be seen as 'competitive' and a way of undermining the full-time parent.

Whatever expectations, attitudes, and practical arrangements are written into the role script for full-time and part-time parents they need to be based on a clear recognition that divorce ends marriage. Only death or very special circumstances should terminate contact between parent and child. Between parent and child, there is no divorce.

## Notes

1. It is assumed that a family is a system consisting of its members with their individual characteristics and all the relationships between them. Suggested reading:
   Barker, P. (1981): *Basic Family Therapy*. London: Granada Publishing Company.
2. Rutter, M., Maughan, B., Mortimore, P. and Ouston, J. (1979): *Fifteen Thousand Hours*. London: Open Books.

3. Rosenshine, B. (1971): *Teaching Behaviour and Student Achievement*. Slough: NFER Publishing Company.
4. Mitchell, A. (1981): *Someone to Turn to*. Aberdeen: Aberdeen University Press.
5. *Marriage Matters* (1979): London: HMSO (Her Majesty's Stationery Office).
6. Lask, J. and Lask, B. (1981): *Child Psychiatry and Social Work*. London: Tavistock Publications.
7. Black, D. (1982): "Custody and Access: A Literary Lesson." *Journal of Family Therapy*, 3; 247–256.
8. Bentovim, A. and Gilmour, L. (1981): "A Family Therapy Interactional Approach to Decision-making in Child Care, Access and Custody Cases." *Journal of Family Therapy*, 3:2, pp 65–77.
9. Caplan, G. (1961): *An Approach to Community Mental Health*. London: Tavistock Publications.
10. Rowlands, P. (1980): *Saturday Parent*. London: George Allen and Unwin.
11. Legislation relating to children of divorcing couples dates back to the Matrimonial Causes Act (1857) which for the first time gave civil courts the right to grant divorce and to make provision for the custody; maintenance and education of the children.

A major step in divorce-related legislation for children was the Guardianship of Infants Act (1925) which introduced the principle of the Welfare of the Child. This was to be of paramount importance in decisions about post-divorce arrangements for children.

The Matrimonial Proceedings (Children) Act (1958) extended the definition of the child of the family to all children of either spouse who had not been accepted as 'a child of the family' by the other. This included natural and adopted children. If suitable arrangements could not be made by the parent/s the court could place a child in the care of the local authority or under supervision. The same Act specified that a court welfare officer should be a probation officer. A decree absolute could not be granted unless a judge was satisfied with the arrangements made for the children.

There has not been any substantial divorce legislation relating to children since 1958. The Divorce Reform Act (1969), since consolidated in the Matrimonial Causes Act (1973), leaves the provisions made for children basically the same as those contained in the 1958 Act.

Under the Matrimonial Causes Rules (1977) a judge or registrar is empowered to call upon a Court Welfare Officer to investigate the circumstances of a divorcing couple with children and report on these to the court.

12. Richards, M. (1981): "Children and the Divorce Courts". *One Parent Times*, No. 7, 2–5. London: National Council for One-Parent Families.
13. Report of the Committee on One-Parent Families (the Finer Report) (1974): London: HMSO.
14. Parkinson, L. (1981): "Joint custody". *One-Parent Times* No 7, 10–13, London: National Council for One-Parent Families.
15. Francis, P. Heygate, S. King, S. and Jones, M. (1983): "Mightier than the Sword", *Social Work Today*, Vol. 14, No 17, 8–10

16. Report of the Committee on One-Parent Families. ibid.
17. The Law Commission (1980): "The Financial Consequences of Divorce: The Basic Policy" (Law Com. No 103) Cmnd. 804. London: HMSO.
18. Study Commission on the Family (1983): *Families in the Future*.
19. Ferri, E. (1976): *Growing Up in a One-Parent Family*. Slough: NFER Publishing Company.
20. The Finer Report, op. cit.
21. Study Commission on the Family, op. cit.
22. Winnicott, D. W. (1968): *The Child, the Family and the Outside World*. Harmondsworth: Penguin Books, 3rd ed.
23. Schaffer, R. (1977): *Mothering*. London: Fontana/Open Books.

Books which may be useful include:
Dr Lee Salk: *What Every Child Should Like his Parents to Know About Divorce*. Harper & Row, 1978.
Anne Hooper: *Divorce and your Children*. George Allen & Unwin, 1981.
Ann Mitchell: *Someone to Turn to – Experience of Help Before Divorce*. Aberdeen University Press, 1981.

Help may be offered to those involved in divorce and with post-divorce problems by the following agencies and groups:
Divorce Conciliation Services – contact the local CAB (Citizens' Advice Bureau) to find out if there is a service in the area.
National Marriage Guidance Council (local branches listed in telephone directory).

Church–based organizations include:
Catholic Marriage Guidance Council, Jewish Marriage Education Council, Westminster Pastoral Foundation.
British Association of Counselling, 1a Little Church Street, Rugby. Tel. 0788 78328
Youth Counselling and Advice Service – contact the CAB for local services.
National Federation of Clubs for the Divorced and Separated, 13 High Street, Little Shelford, Cambridge CB2 5BS. These can be contacted for information about local clubs.
Family Welfare Association Private Counselling Service, London. North London, Tel. 273 5173; South London, Tel. 699 4262.
Families Need Fathers, 37 Carden Road, London, SE15. Help for non-custodial parents.
National Council for One-Parent Families, 255 Kentish Town Road, London NW5.
Gingerbread. The central office is at 35 Wellington Street, London WC2 and may be contacted for information about local groups. Self-help association for one-parent families.

# BIBLIOGRAPHY

Anderson, H. (1977): 'Children of Divorce'. *Journal of Clinical Psychology*, Vol 6. 41–43. Brandon, U.S.A.: The Clinical Psychology Publishing Corporation.

Barker, P. (1981): *Basic Family Therapy*. London: Granada.

Beard, R. M. (1969): *An Outline of Piaget's Developmental Psychology*. London: Routledge and Kegan Paul.

Bee, H. (1974): *Social Issues in Developmental Psychology*. London: Harper and Row.

Bee, H. and Mitchell, S. K. (1980): *The Developing Person*. London: Harper and Row.

Bentovim, A. and Gilmour, L. (1981): 'A Family Therapy Interactional Approach to Decision-making in Child Care, Access and Custody Cases'. *Journal of Family Therapy*, Vol. 3, No. 2: 65–77. London: Academic Press.

Black, D. (1982): 'Custody and Access; a Literary Lesson'. *Journal of Family Therapy*, Vol. 4, no. 3: 247–256. London: Academic Press.

Bowlby, J. (1969): 'Attachment and Loss', Vol. I. *Attachment*. London: Hogarth Press.

Bowlby, J. (1973): 'Attachment and Loss', Vol II. *Separation: Anxiety and Anger*. London: Hogarth Press.

Bowlby, J. (1979): *The Making and Breaking of Affectional Bonds*. London: Tavistock Publications.

Bowlby, J. (1980): 'Attachment and Loss', Vol. 3. *Loss, Sadness and Depression*. London: Hogarth Press.

Brown, J. W. and Harris, T. (1978): *Social Origins of Depression*. London: Tavistock Publications.

Burgoine, J. and Clarke, D. (1982): Reconstituted Families in Rapoport R. N. Fogarty, M. P. and Rapoport R. (ed) Families in Britain, London, for British Commission on Family Research, Routledge and Kegan Paul.

Burnell, I, and Wadsworth, J. (1982): 'Home Truths', *One-Parent Times*, 8: 8–12. London: National Council for One-Parent Families.

Caplan, G. (1961): *An Approach to Community Mental Health*. London: Tavistock Publications.

Carroll, Lewis (1865): *Alice's Adventures in Wonderland* (1946). Harmondsworth: Penguin Books.

Central Statistical Office, Social Trends (1980), Vol. 11 (1981): Vol. 12 (1982); Vol. 13, London: HMSO.

Clarke, A. M. and Clarke, A. D. B. (1976): *Early Experience, Myth and Evidence*. London: Open Books.

Corman, Avery (1978): *Kramer* v. *Kramer*. Glasgow: William Collins, Sons and Co Ltd.

Davie, R. Butler, N. R. and Goldstein, H. (1972): *From Birth to Seven*. London: Longman in association with National Children's Bureau.

Department of Health and Social Security: Committee on One Parent Families, Chairman Sir Morris Finer (1974): *Report of the Committee on One Parent Families*. 2 volumes. London: HMSO.

Dlugokinski, E. (1977): 'A Developmental Approach to Coping with Divorce', *Journal of Clinical Child Psychology* 6: 27–30 Brandon, U.S.A. The Clinical Psychology Publishing Corporation.

Eekelar, J. and Clive, E. (1977): *Custody after Divorce: The Disposition of Custody in Divorce Cases in Great Britain*. Centre for Socio-legal Studies: Wolfson College, Oxford.

Essen, J. and Lambert, L. (1977): 'Living in one-parent families: relationships and attitudes of 16-year olds.' Child: care, health and development 3: 301–318 London, National Children's Bureaux.

Ferri, E. (1976): *Growing up in One-Parent Family: A Long-Term Study of Child Development*. Windsor: NFER Publishing Company.

Ferri, E. and Robinson, H. (1976): *Coping Alone*. Windsor: NFER Publishing Company.

Fogelman, K. R. (ed) (1976): *Britain's Sixteen-Year-Olds*. London: National Children's Bureaux.

Francis, P. Heygate, S. King, S. and Jones, M. (1983): 'Mightier than the Sword', *Social Work Today* Vol. 14, No 17: 8–10. British Association of Social Workers, Birmingham.

Fraser, R. D. (1980): 'Divorce Avon style – the Work of a Specialist Welfare Team'. *Social Work Today*, Vol. 11, No 30: 13–15. British Association of Social Workers, Birmingham.

Freud, S. (1953–1964): *The Standard Edition of the Complete Psychological Works of Sigmund Freud*. Strachey, J. (ed). London: Hogarth Press.

Galper, M. (1978): *Co-parenting (Sharing your Child Equally)*. Philadelphia: Running Press.

Gardner, A. (1977): 'Children of Divorce – Some Legal and Psychological Considerations'. *Journal of Clinical Child Psychology*, Vol 6: 3–6. Brandon, U.S.A: The Clinical Psychology Publishing Corporation.

Gardner, G. (1978): *Social Surveys for Social Planners*: Milton Keynes: Open University Press.

George, V. and Wilding, P. (1972): *Motherless Families*. London: Routledge and Kegan Paul.

Goldstein, J. Freud, A. and Solnit, A. J. (1973): *Before the Best Interests of the Child*: London: Collier MacMillan.

Goode, Wm. (1956): *After Divorce*. New York, Free Press, reprinted (1956) as *Women in Divorce*, New York, Free Press.

Graham, Hall, J. (1976): 'The Case for Conciliation Bureaux.' Chichester: *Family Law*, Vol. 6, No. 8: 231–236.

Green, Maureen (1976): *Goodbye Father*. London: Routledge and Kegan Paul.

Grollman, E. A. and Grollman, S. H. (1977): 'How to Tell Children About Divorce'. *Journal of Clinical Child Psychology* Vol. 6, 35–37. Brandon, USA: The Clinical Psychology Publishing Corporation.

Haddad, R. M. (1978): *The Disposable Parent: The Case for Joint Custody*. New York, Penguin Books.

Hall, A. D. and Fagan, R. E. (1956): 'Definition of System, in General Systems': *Yearbook of the Society for the Advancement of General Systems Theory*. L. von Bertalanffy, and Rapoport, A. (eds), New York.

Hall, C. S. (1954): *A Primer of Freudian Psychology*. New York: New American Library.

Hart, N. (1976): *When Marriage Ends: A Study in Status Passage*. London: Tavistock Publications.

Hess, R. D. and Camara, D. A. (1979): 'Post-divorce Relationships as Mediating Factors in the Consequences of Divorce for Children'. *Journal of Social Issues*, Vol. 35, No. 4: 79–96. Ann Arbor, USA. Society for the Psychological Study of Social Issues.

Hetherington, E. M. Cox, M. and Cox, R. (1978): 'The Aftermath of Divorce' in Stevens, Jr. J. H. and Mathews, M. (eds). *Mother-Child, Father-Child Relations*. Washington D. C: National Association for the Education of Young Children.

Hetherington, E. M, Cox, M. and Cox, R. (1979): 'Play and Social Interaction in Children Following Divorce.' *Journal of Social Issues*, 35, 26–49.

Home Office (1979): *Marriage Matters*. London: HMSO.

Hooper, A. (1981): Divorce and Your Children. London: George Allen and Unwin.

Hunt, M. (1966): *The World of the Formerly Married*. New York: McGraw-Hill.

Ingliss, R. (1982): *Must Divorce Hurt the Children?* London: Maurice Temple Smith.

James, Henry (1897): *What Maisie Knew*. Jefferson, D. and Grant, D. (eds), (1982) edition, World's Classic paperbacks, Oxford: Oxford University Press.

Kellmer Pringle, M. (1975), 4th ed (1982): *The Needs of Children*. London: Hutchinson.

Klein, M. and others (1952): *Developments in Psychoanalysis*: Rivière, J. (ed). London: Hogarth Press.

Klein, M. (1975): *The Writings of Melanie Klein*, Vols. 1–4, London: Hogarth Press.

Lambert, L. (1978): 'Living in One-parent Families: School-leavers and Their Future.' *Concern*, No. 29, Autumn 1978. 26–30, London: National Children's Bureaux.

Lask, J. and Lask, B. (1981): *Child Psychiatry and Social Work*. London: Tavistock Publications.

Leonard, Barker, D. and Allen, S. (1976): *Dependence and Exploitation in Work and Marriage*. London: Longman.

Maidment, S. (1976): 'A Study in Child Custody,' part I, *Family Law*, Vol. 6, No. 7: 195–200, Chichester.

Maddox, B. (1975): *The Half Parent*, London: André Deutsch (1980): *Step-Parenting*. London: Unwin paperbacks.

Marsden, C. (1969): *Mothers Alone: Poverty and the Fatherless Family*, London: Allen Lane.

Mathews, T. J. (1977): "Beyond Divorce: The Impact of Remarriage on Children". *Journal of Clinical Psychology*. 6. 59–61. Brandon USA. The Clinical Psychology Publishing Corporation.

Mitchell, A. K. (1981): *Someone to Talk to*. Aberdeen: Aberdeen University Press.

Mortlake, B. (1972): *The Inside of Divorce*. London: Constable.

Murch, M. (1977): 'The Role of Solicitors in Divorce Proceedings'. *Modern Law Review* 40: 625–638 and (1978) 41: 25–37. London: Stevens and Sons Ltd.

*National Council for One Parent Families Annual Reports*, 1980, 1981, 1982. London: National Council for One Parent Families.

Nerls, N. and Morgenbesser, M. (1980): 'Joint Custody: An Exploration of the Issue,' *Family Process* 19: 117–125.

Opie, I. and Opie, P. (1963): *The Puffin Book of Nursery Rhymes*. Harmondsworth: Puffin Books.

Parke, R. D. (1981): *Fathering*. London: Fontana.

Parkes, C. M. (1972): *Bereavement: Studies of Grief in Adult Life*. London: Tavistock Publications.

Parkinson, L. (1981): 'Joint Custody'. *One Parent Times*, No. 7. 10–13. London: National Council for One Parent Families.

Parsons, Talcott, and Bales, R. F. (1956): *Family: Socialisation and Interaction Process*. London: Routledge and Kegan Paul.

Piaget, J. (1953): *The Origins of Intelligence in the Child*. London: Routledge and Kegan Paul.

Pincus, L. and Dare, C. (1978): *Secrets in the Family*. London: Faber and Faber.

Rapoport, L. (1965): 'The State of Crisis – Some Theoretical Considerations', in Parad, H. J. (ed). *Crisis Intervention*. New York: Family Service Association of America.

Reinhard, D. W. (1977): 'The Reactions of Adolescent Boys and Girls to the Divorce of Their Parents'. *Journal of Clinical Psychology*, Vol. 6, 21–23. Brandon, USA: The Clinical Psychology Publishing Corporation.

Richards, M. (1976): *The Integration of a Child into a Social World*, 3rd edition. Cambridge: Cambridge University Press.

Richards, M. (1980): *Infancy*. London: Harper and Row.

Richards, M. (1981): 'Children and the Divorce Courts'. *One Parent Times*, No. 7, 2–5. London: National Council for One Parent Families.

Robinson, M. (1980): 'Step-families: A Reconstituted Family System.' *Journal of Family Therapy*, Vol. 2, No. 1, 45–69. London: Academic Press.

Rosen, R. (1977): 'Children of Divorce: What They Feel about Access and Other Aspects of the Divorce Experience'. *Journal of Clinical Child Psychology*, Vol. 6, 24–27. Brandon, USA: The Clinical Psychology Publishing Corporation.

Rosenshine, B. (1971): *Teaching Behaviour and Student Achievement*. Slough: NFER Publishing Company.

Rowlands, P. (1980): *Saturday Parent*. London: George Allen and Unwin.

Rutter, M. (1971): 'Parent-Child Separation: Psychological Effects on Children.' *Journal of Child Psychology and Psychiatry*, Vol 12, 233–260. Oxford, Pergamon Press.

Rutter, M. (1972): *Maternal Deprivation Reassessed*. Harmondsworth: Penguin Books.

Rutter, M. Maughan, B. Mortimore, P. and Ouston, J. (1979): *Fifteen Thousand Hours*. London: Open Books.

Salk, L. (1977): 'On the Custody Rights of Fathers in Divorce'. *Journal of Clinical Psychology*, Vol. 6, 49–50. Brendon, U.S.A: The Clinical Psychology Publishing Corporation.

Salk, L. (1978): *What Every Child Should Like His Parents to Know About Divorce*. London: Harper and Row.

Satir, V. (1964): *Conjoint Family Therapy*. Palo Alto: Science and Behaviour Books.

Satir, V. (1972): *People Making Palo Alto*. Palo Alto: Science and Behaviour Books.

Schaffer, R. (1977): *Mothering*. London: Fontana/Open Books.

Seagull, A. and Seagull, E. (1977): 'The Non-custodial Father's Relationship to his Child: Conflicts and Solutions'. *Journal of Clinical Psychology* Vol. 6, 11–15. Brandon, USA: The Clinical Psychology Publishing Corporation.

Segal, H. (1979): *Klein*. London. Fontana/Collins.

Seligman, M. E. P. (1975): *Helplessness: on Depression, Development and Death*. San Francisco. Freeman.

Study Commission on the Family (1983): *Families in the Future*. London.

Tolstoy, L. *Anna Karenina*, English Translation (1960): London: Everyman's Library, Dent.

Wallerstein, J. S. and Kelly, J. B. (1975): 'The Effects of Parental Divorce on the Preschool Child'. *American Academy of Child Psychiatry Journal*, Vol. 14, 4: 600–617.

Wallerstein, J. S. and Kelly, J. B. (1979): 'Children and Divorce; A Review'. *Social Work*, 24, 468–475.

Wallerstein J. S. and Kelly, J. B. (1982): *Surviving the Breakup; How Children and Parents Cope with Divorce*. Grant McIntyre. New York: Basic Books.

Walrond-Skinner, S. (1976): *Family Therapy: The Treatment of Natural Systems*. London: Routledge and Kegan Paul.

Weiss, R. S. (1975): *Marital Separation*. New York: Basic Books.

Wilkinson, M. (1981): *Children and Divorce*. Oxford: Basil Blackwell.

Winnicott, D. W. (1964): *The Child, the Family and the Outside World*. Harmondsworth, Penguin Books.

Winnicott, D. W. (1965): *The Family and Individual Development*. London: Tavistock Publications.

# APPENDIX

## Interviewing Schedule

1 **Age**
    a Now
    b When parents separated
    c When parents divorced

2 **Family structure**
Members of the family and ages at time of separation.

3 **Occupation**
    a Child
    b Mother
    c Father

4 **Education of child**
    a School (type)
    b Further education

5 **Where born** (Town and Country)
    a Child
    b Mother
    c Father

6 **How do you think your parents got on while they were together?**

7 **What are your childhood memories?**
How did you get on
    a With mother    b With father
    c With siblings    d With others

e  With friends

g  Restrictions

f  At school

h  How do you remember yourself as a child (e.g., lively,
happy, lonely, shy).

8  **Circumstances of parting**
e.g., What actually happened

9  **Why did/do you think the marriage ended?**

10  **What were your feelings and reactions at the time of separation and subsequently?**

11  **What were you told? and by whom?**

12  **What did you find out for yourself?**
(e.g., through overhearing conversations)

13  **Did you take any action?**
(e.g., attempt a reconciliation, run away, inform others)

14  **Since your parents separated and until now (or your 18th birthday, if over 18), with whom do/did you live?**

15  **What arrangements were made for you (following separation and until your 18th birthday)?**
a  Custody
c  Financial
b  Care and control
d  Access (e.g., visiting, staying, etc)

16  **Were you and did you wish to be consulted?**

17  **What are/were your view and feelings about these arrangements?**
a  Immediately following separation
b  In the long run

18  **In connection with your parents' separation and divorce, did you get any help from**
a  Parents
c  Social workers
e  Others
b  Relatives and friends
d  Teachers

19    **If yes, what did you think of it?**

20    **If no, what help would you have liked?**

21    **As a result of separation in what way, if any, has the relationship changed with**
     a Mother                b Father
     c Siblings             d Others

22    **Finance: as a result of your parents' separation, were you**
     a Better off
     b Worse off
     c The same
Give your reasons

23    **Has either parent remarried or had other relationships?**
     If yes
     a In what circumstances?
     b What did/do you feel about it?

24    **How do/did you get on with parents'**
     a Spouses
     b Other partners

25    **What lasting effect do you think your parents' separation and divorce have had on you, if any?**

26    **Are there any additional comments you wish to make?**

# AUTHOR INDEX

# SUBJECT INDEX